D1941575

REWARD

Elementary

Practice Book

Diana Pye
Simon Greenall

MACMILLAN
HEINEMANN
English Language Teaching

Hueber

1 What's your name?

VOCABULARY

1 Welche Stadt gehört zu welchem Land?

Rome	Australia
Rio de Janeiro	Russia
Washington	Turkey
Moscow	Italy
Sydney	the United States of America
Istanbul	Brazil

2 Suchen Sie 17 Länder in diesem Rätsel. Die Wörter können in zwei Richtungen gelesen werden (→) und (↓).

S	P	A	I	N	I	N	D	I	A
P	A	R	G	E	N	T	I	N	A
E	G	F	T	U	R	K	E	Y	T
R	R	R	C	I	U	O	B	Y	H
U	E	A	H	T	S	R	R	M	A
J	E	N	I	A	S	E	I	E	I
A	C	C	N	L	I	A	T	X	L
P	E	E	A	Y	A	I	A	I	A
A	C	A	N	A	D	A	I	C	N
N	B	R	A	Z	I	L	N	O	D

3 Zu welchen sechs Ländern aus dem Rätsel gehören diese Städte? Bilden Sie Sätze.

Madrid Seoul Buenos Aires Paris Tokyo Athens Lima

Madrid is in Spain.

1. Seoul is in Korea.
2. Buenos Aieres is in
3. Paris is in France.
4. Tokyo is in Japan.
5. Athens is in Greece.
6. Lima is in Peru.

FUNCTIONS

1 Bringen Sie diese Wörter in die richtige Reihenfolge, um Sätze zu bilden.

1. what your is name?
   What is your name?
2. from where you are?
   Where are you from?
3. is my Charlie name.
   My name is Charlie.
4. from am I Canada.
   I am from Canada.
5. name Maria your is?
   Is your name Maria?

2 Zu welcher Frage in Übung 1 passen jeweils diese Antworten.

a. No, my name's Anna. 5
b. My name's Juan. 1
c. I'm from the United States. 2

3 Beantworten Sie die Fragen in Übung 1.

1. I'm Lucy. / My name is Lucy
2. I'm from Slovakia.
3. No, my name is Lucy.

4 Unterstreichen Sie die Verben. Machen Sie einen Kreis um die Subjektpronomen.

is what your the am Mary from name you where I are hello my Brazil be yes

5 Bilden Sie fünf Sätze mit den Wörtern aus Übung 4.

1. Where are you from?
2. I am from Brazil.
3. What is your Name?
4. My name is Mary.
5.

SOUNDS

1 Hören Sie zu und machen Sie ein Häkchen neben die Länder, die erwähnt werden.

China Japan Turkey Italy Brazil Mexico
Hungary Spain Britain Germany Russia Korea
Thailand Canada Ukraine Poland Morocco

2 Reihen Sie die in Übung 1 abgehakten Länder in die richtige Spalte ein.

o O	O o	O o o	o O o
	China		

Hören Sie noch einmal zu und kontrollieren Sie.

LISTENING

1 Sie hören nun vier Gespräche. Welches Gespräch passt zu welchem Bild?

A ☐

B ☐ C ☐ D ☐

2 Hören Sie noch einmal zu und ergänzen Sie die Gespräche mit diesen Ländern.

1 the United States of America
2 Italy
3 Australia
4 Spain
5 Canada
6 Britain
7 Sweden
8 France

Conversation 1

A Hello, I'm Juan.
B Hello, Juan. My name's Anna. I'm from ______________ . Where are you from, Juan?
A I'm from ______________ .

Conversation 2

C Hello, my name's Thomas, Peter Thomas.
D Hello, Mr Thomas. I'm Marco Placidi. I'm from ______________ . Where are you from?
C I'm from ____________________________ .

Conversation 3

E Hello, I'm Ingrid. What's your name?
F Hello, Ingrid. My name's Sally. Where are you from?
E I'm from ______________. And you, Sally? Where are you from?
F I'm from ______________ .

Conversation 4

G Hello, my name's Janet Smith.
H Hello, Mrs Smith. I'm Marilyn Kelly.
G Where are you from, Mrs Kelly?
H I'm from ______________ .

2 This is Bruno and Maria

VOCABULARY

1 Unterstreichen Sie die Berufe.

teacher student town name waiter where receptionist country tourist doctor chef nationality actor artist police officer nurse their journalist

2 Schauen Sie sich die Bilder an. Welche Berufe haben diese Menschen? Bilden Sie Sätze.

1 He's a waiter.
2 She's an artist.
3 He's a chef.
4 She's a nurse.
5 He's a vet.
6 They're police officers.

3 Unterstreichen Sie jeweils das Wort, das nicht zu den anderen passt.

1 he she her you they
2 Brazil Croatia Moscow Greece China
3 my we our their his
4 Prague Seoul Ankara Brazil Madrid
5 friend teacher journalist technician accountant
6 I'm your he's she's you're

4 Bilden Sie Sätze mit den unterstrichenen Wörtern.

1 *Her name is Helena.*
2
3
4
5
6

GRAMMAR

1 Unterstreichen Sie die richtige Form.

1 *They're/Their* German.
2 *You're/Your* from Barcelona.
3 *They're/Their* friend is a doctor.
4 What nationality is *you're/your* friend?
5 *They're/Their* parents are from Poland.

2 Ergänzen Sie diese Sätze mit *his* oder *he's*.

1 He's from Mexico.
2 His name is Karl.
3 He's Italian.
4 What's his name?
5 He's a student.

3 Ersetzen Sie die Namen durch ein Pronomen.

Artur is from Poland.
He's from Poland.

1 Maria is a secretary.
She's a secretary.

2 John and Chrissie are from Australia.
They're from A.

3 Kevin is an actor.
He's –||–

4 Paul and Karl are doctors.
They're doctors.

5 My brother and I are farmers.
We're farmers.

4 **Schreiben Sie jeweils die unverkürzte Form des Verbs auf.**

What's your name?
What is your name?

1 He's a teacher.
He is a teacher.

2 They're from Thailand.
They are from Thailand.

3 I'm Spanish.
I am Spanish.

4 We're students.
We are students.

5 They're actors.
They are actors.

6 She's a doctor.
She is a doctor.

READING

1 **Lesen Sie die Beschreibungen. Welche Berufe haben diese Menschen? Bilden Sie Sätze.**

1 *Maria is a receptionist.*
2 Jim is a jazz musician.
3 Isabella is an economist.
4 Yannick is a journalist.
5 Emma is a nurse.

A My name is Maria. I'm from Milan and I'm Italian. I'm a receptionist in a hotel in London. My boyfriend is British. His name is Jim and he's a jazz musician.

B My name is Yannick. I'm from France. I'm a journalist for an international magazine. My wife's name is Isabella and she's from Barcelona. She's an economist.

C I'm Emma Simpson. I'm a nurse in Edinburgh but I'm from London. My parents are teachers at the university here.

2 **Korrigieren Sie diese Sätze.**

1 Yannick is from Spain.
Yannick isn't from Spain, he is from France.

2 Maria is from London.
Maria isn't from London, she is from Italia.

3 Emma is a student.
Emma isn't a student, she is a nurse.

4 Jim is an actor.
Jim isn't an actor, he is a jazz musician.

5 Emma's parents are doctors.
Emma's parents aren't doctors, they are teachers.

3 **Schreiben Sie die Beschreibung B noch einmal neu in der dritten Person.**

His name is Yannick.

LISTENING

1 **Hören Sie sich das Gespräch an. Unterstreichen Sie die Wörter, die nicht mit dem Gespräch übereinstimmen.**

A Hi there. My name's Jan. I'm from Britain. I'm a computer technician here at the university.
B Hello, Jan. My name's Lee. I'm from Vancouver in Canada. I'm a student.
A This is my friend, Sara. She's from France. She's a teacher.
B Hello, Sara.
C Hello, Lee.

2 **Ergänzen Sie das Gespräch mit *his*, *he's* oder *he*.**

A Hello, Peter. What's your friend's name?
B He name's Silvio.
A Where's he from?
B He's from Italy.
A What's his job?
B He's an accountant.

Hören Sie zu und kontrollieren Sie.

3 Questions, questions

VOCABULARY

1 Machen Sie einen Kreis um die Substantive (Hauptwörter). Unterstreichen Sie die Adjektive (Eigenschaftswörter).

married student his children are her
Japan there from doctor single surname
phone number he brother is actor not am
friend where good-looking address
first name what job boyfriend

2 Bilden Sie Sätze mit fünf Substantiven aus Übung 1.

1 ______
2 ______
3 ______
4 ______
5 ______

GRAMMAR

1 Welche Antwort passt zu welcher Frage?

1 How old is he? c
2 What's her job? d
3 Who's this? e
4 Where are you from? a
5 What's your telephone number? f
6 How are you? b

a Rosslare in Ireland.
b Fine, thanks.
c He's thirteen years old.
d She's a nurse.
e Ann Smith.
f 01478 859 321.

2 Ergänzen Sie die Sätze mit einem Fragewort: *What, Where, How* oder *Who*.

1 Where are you from?
2 How old are you?
3 What is your address?
4 Who is your favourite actor?
5 Where is your home?
6 What is your telephone number?

3 Beantworten Sie die Fragen in Übung 2.

1 I'm from Slovakia.
2 I'm 30
3 My address is ...
4 My favorite actor is Nicolas Cage.
5 My home is in Fellbach
6 My telephone number is ...

4 Schreiben Sie passende Fragen zu den folgenden Antworten.

1 Have she a boyfriend? / Is she married?
No, she's single.
2 Are you single?
No, I'm married.
3 Are his children medical students.
Yes, his children are medical students.
4 Is he from Manchaster?
No, he isn't, he's from London.
5 Are you a vet?
No, I'm a journalist.
6 Is she a French teacher at the university?
Yes, she's a French teacher at the university.

5 Widersprechen Sie diesen Behauptungen.

He's from London. (Oxford)
No, he isn't. He's from Oxford.
1 She's from Hungary. (Romania)
No, she isn't. She's from Romania.
2 He's a doctor. (nurse)
No, he isn't. He's a nurse.
3 They're Spanish. (Argentinian)
No, they aren't. They're Argentinian.
4 She's eighteen. (seventeen)
No, she isn't. She's seventeen.
5 He's single. (married)
No, he isn't. He's married.

SOUNDS

Hören Sie sich die Fragen aus GRAMMAR Übung 2 an. Achten Sie auf die Betonung.

Hören Sie noch einmal zu und wiederholen Sie.

LISTENING

1 Hören Sie sich das folgende Gespräch an. Wo findet das Gespräch statt?

at the doctor's ☐ at the police station ☐

at a job interview ☐ at a business meeting ☐

2 Hören Sie noch einmal zu. Schreiben Sie vier Fragen auf, die vom Interviewer gestellt werden.

1 ________________

2 ________________

3 ________________

4 ________________

3 Korrigieren Sie diese Sätze.

Maria is a hotel manager.

No, she isn't. She's a receptionist.

1 Maria is married.

No, she isn't. She's a single.

2 Maria is twenty years old.

____

3 Maria is British.

____

WRITING

1 Welche der abgebildeten Personen passt zu welchem Passeintrag? Eine Person bleibt übrig.

2 Beschreiben Sie zwei der abgebildeten Personen.

____

____

____

____

____

____

____

____

A

B

C

D

SURNAME	Haines
FIRST NAME	Michael
ADDRESS	3, End Street, Cardiff
DATE OF BIRTH	12 November 1942
PLACE OF BIRTH	Bristol
SEX	M
CHILDREN	2
OCCUPATION	Airline pilot

SURNAME	Singh
FIRST NAME	Janvi
ADDRESS	24, Thames Road, Reading
DATE OF BIRTH	3 May 1967
PLACE OF BIRTH	London
SEX	F
CHILDREN	None
OCCUPATION	Doctor

SURNAME	Downs
FIRST NAME	May
ADDRESS	Grove Cottage, Hay
DATE OF BIRTH	14 January 1927
PLACE OF BIRTH	Bristol
SEX	F
CHILDREN	5
OCCUPATION	Retired

4 How many students are there?

VOCABULARY

1 Unterstreichen Sie jeweils das Wort, das nicht zu den anderen passt.

1 kind lovely room friendly good
2 eight twelve chair fifty nine
3 interesting book room school computer
4 where how who what that

2 Bilden Sie Sätze mit den unterstrichenen Wörtern aus Übung 1.

1 ______
2 ______
3 ______
4 ______

3 Ergänzen Sie die Sätze mit einem der folgenden Adjektive.

good beautiful comfortable kind interesting

1 He's a kind man.
2 She's a good teacher.
3 It's an interesting lesson.
4 It's a comfortable chair.
5 It's a beatiful city.

GRAMMAR AND SOUNDS

1 Hören Sie zu und schreiben Sie die Zahlen auf.

______
______
______

Sprechen Sie alle Zahlen laut.

2 Schreiben Sie die Mehrzahl-Form dieser Wörter auf.

classroom	clasrooms
teacher	teachers
address	addresses
number	numbers
college	colleges
class	classes
chair	chairs

Hören Sie zu und kontrollieren Sie. Sprechen Sie die Wörter laut.

3 Bilden Sie Sätze mit *there is* oder *there are*.

thirty desks in the room
There are thirty desks in the room.

1 a book and a pen on the table
There is one book & one pen on the table.
2 three students in the classroom
There are three students in the classroom.
3 a computer on the table
There is one computer on the table.
4 two good schools in the town
There are 2 good schools in the town.
5 a cassette player in the room
There is one cassette player in the room.

4 Hören Sie zu und ordnen Sie die th-Wörter in zwei Gruppen ein.

thirteen this their three with there thanks the they think

/θ/ *thirteen*
______

/ð/ *this*
______

READING

1 Lesen Sie die Beschreibung einer Schule. Um welche Art Schule handelt es sich?

bilingual school

2 Unterstreichen Sie die Adjektive im Text.

3 Beantworten Sie die Fragen.

1 Is it a big school?
No, isn't a very big school.

2 Is it for adults or children?
It's for children.

3 How old are the writer's children?
The writer's children are from six to ten years of age.

4 Where is the school?
The school is in the town centre.

5 Is it a very modern school?
It's very modern school.

My two children are at a new bilingual school in the town centre. There are English and Italian children in each class. The lessons are in English and Italian. The school is in an old building but the classrooms are very modern. It's not a very big school. There are fifty pupils from six to ten years of age. There are four classes. The teachers are very friendly and their English is very good. My children are six and nine years old. The classrooms are big and comfortable. There's a big library with a television and video. There's also a special room with twelve computers. There's a small garden for the children. It's a very good school but it's also a very expensive school.

WRITING

1 Schauen Sie sich den Text im Abschnitt READING noch einmal an. Beschreiben Sie Ihre Schule in ähnlicher Weise.

2 Lesen Sie diese Sätze. Machen Sie ein Häkchen neben die Sätze, die auch Ihr Klassenzimmer beschreiben.

1 It's big and comfortable. ☐
2 It isn't very modern. ☐
3 There are tables and chairs. ☐
4 There isn't a computer. ☐
5 There is a tape recorder. ☐
6 There is a blackboard. ☐
7 There is a big window. ☐
8 There is a television and video. ☐

3 Beschreiben Sie Ihr Klassenzimmer in ein paar Sätzen.

5 Where's my pen?

VOCABULARY

1 Ordnen Sie die Wörter in die richtigen Kategorien ein.

accountant calculator camera city computer country diary doctor farmer library mobile phone notebook pen pencil personal stereo radio school vet

Electronic products: ____________

Office things: ____________

Jobs: ____________

Places: ____________

2 Wie heißen die abgebildeten Gegenstände?

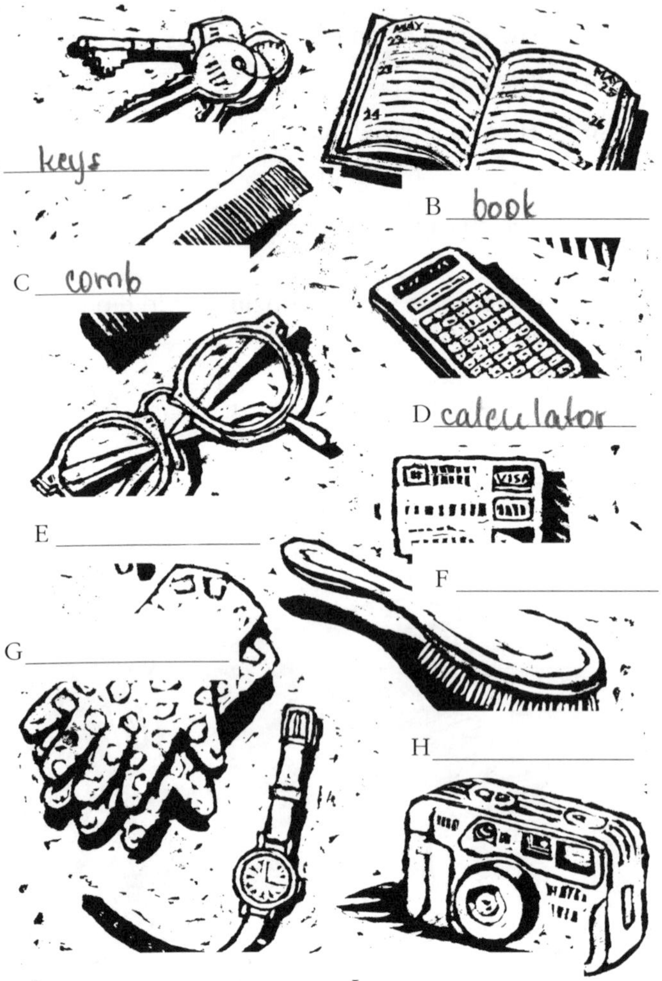

A keys

B book

C comb

D calculator

E ____________

F ____________

G ____________

H ____________

I ____________

J ____________

3 Ordnen Sie die richtige Präposition (Verhältniswort) zu.

on under in near

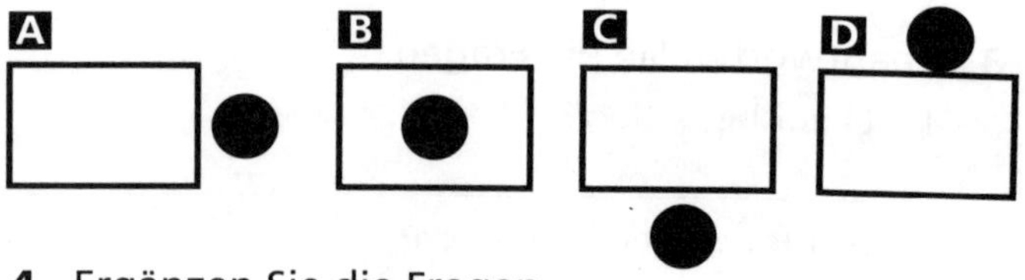

4 Ergänzen Sie die Fragen.

Where What How

1 ____________ do you spell *wallet*?

2 ____________ is this in English?

3 ____________ colour is your bag?

4 ____________ is your pen?

GRAMMAR

1 Schreiben Sie die Sätze ohne die Verkürzungen noch einmal neu.

We're from London.

We are from London.

1 He's got a new video.

2 They've got a television and a video.

3 She's a secretary at the bank.

4 I've got a hat and gloves in my bag.

5 She's got a mobile phone in her bag.

6 He's twenty-five years old today.

2 Was haben Sie bei sich? Schreiben Sie fünf Sätze.

I've got three keys.

1 ____________

2 ____________

3 ____________

4 ____________

5 ____________

3 Wo sind sie? Bilden Sie Sätze.

your car

It's in the car park.

1 your diary

____

2 your telephone

____

3 your Student's Book

____

4 your bag

____

5 your coat

____

SOUNDS

1 Hören Sie zu und schreiben Sie die Wörter auf.

1 _ A _ _ E T	4 _ _ _ E R _
2 _ _ L O U _	5 W _ _ _ H
3 _ _ M B	6 _ I _ R _

2 Hören Sie zu. Beachten Sie die Aussprache der unterstrichenen Buchstaben.

1 It's the black key.
2 He's got a pink car.
3 I've got a black coat.
4 He's got a red telephone.
5 There's a red diary on the table.

Hören Sie noch einmal zu und wiederholen Sie.

3 Hören Sie zu und wiederholen Sie.

radio stereo video phone mobile coat comb

LISTENING

Hören Sie sich das Gespräch an und ergänzen Sie es.

A Where are my __________?
B What __________ are they?
A __________ and __________. They're not in my __________.
B Well, they're not __________ the table. Are they __________ your book?
A Oh, yes. Here they are. Thanks.

WRITING

Beschreiben Sie das Zimmer.

____
____
____
____
____
____
____
____
____
____

6 Families

VOCABULARY

1 Ergänzen Sie die Aufstellung.

Male	**Female**
man	______________
______________	girl
father	______________
______________	sister
______________	niece
son	______________
husband	______________
______________	aunt
grandfather	______________
cousin	______________

2 Ergänzen Sie die Sätze mit Wörtern aus der Aufstellung in Übung 1.

1 My mother's sister is my ____________.
2 My brother's daughter is my ____________.
3 My father's mother is my ____________.
4 My daughter's brother is my ____________.
5 My mother and father's son is my ____________.
6 My aunt's son is my ____________.

3 Schreiben Sie die Mehrzahl-Formen auf.

man ______________________________
woman ______________________________
child ______________________________
family ______________________________
person ______________________________
wife ______________________________
country ______________________________

READING AND GRAMMAR

1 Schauen Sie sich die Bilder an. Beschreiben Sie die Familien in ein paar Sätzen.

Family A:
There are four people in the family.
____
____

Family B:
____
____

2 In diesem Text sind die Beschreibungen der zwei abgebildeten Familien durcheinander gebracht worden. Lesen Sie den Text und unterstreichen Sie alles, was zur Beschreibung von Familie A gehört.

Jenny is thirty-two years old and has got a job in a post office in a small village. Peter is thirty-nine years old and he is an architect in London. He is married to Elizabeth and they've got four children: three sons and a daughter. She's divorced and has got an eight-year-old daughter, Cilla, and a three-year-old son, Jamie. She's got a small house with a big garden in the village. They live in a big house near London. She's got a lot of friends in the village. Elizabeth looks after the children and has a part-time job in a school near her home. Jenny's mother, Kate, lives in the same village. Peter's parents, Fiona and Michael, live in the country and come to stay with the family in the holidays. They have a comfortable life and they are a happy family. She helps Jenny with the children when she's at work.

3 Korrigieren Sie die falschen Aussagen.

1 Jenny's husband is Peter.

____

2 Elizabeth is an architect.

____

3 Peter has got two children.

____

4 Jenny has got a part-time job in a school.

____

5 Jenny has got a house near London.

____

4 Wer sind diese Personen?

Kate *is Jenny's mother.*

1 Elizabeth

____

2 Fiona and Michael

____

3 Cilla

____

4 Jamie

____

5 Schauen Sie sich diesen Stammbaum an. Beschreiben Sie die verwandtschaftlichen Beziehungen. Bilden Sie Sätze.

Helen is John's grandmother.

Jane has got one brother and two cousins.

____

____

____

____

____

____

____

LISTENING

1 Schauen Sie sich den Stammbaum in GRAMMAR Übung 5 an. Hören Sie zu, wie zwei der abgebildeten Personen ihre Familie beschreiben. Wer spricht?

Speaker 1: ______________________

Speaker 2: ______________________

2 Hören Sie noch einmal zu. Ergänzen Sie die Informationen über die Familienmitglieder.

1 Sally has got an interesting job; she's a ____________.

2 Philippa is ____________ years old.

3 Greg is not British, he's ____________.

4 Greg has got a job with a ____________ company.

5 Henry is not ____________.

WRITING

Zeichnen Sie Ihren eigenen Stammbaum. Beschreiben Sie in ein paar Sätzen Ihre Verwandtschaft.

____

____

____

____

____

____

____

____

____

____

7 What's the time?

VOCABULARY

1 Wieviel Uhr ist es?

3.30 pm: *It's half past three in the afternoon.*

1 4.20 pm: ______

2 10.45 am: ______

3 9.00 pm: ______

4 11.30 am: ______

5 6.15 am: ______

2 Bringen Sie diese Tätigkeiten in die richtige Reihenfolge. Nummerieren Sie die Kästchen entsprechend.

have lunch ☐

go to bed ☐

finish work ☐

have breakfast ☐

start work ☐

have dinner ☐

get up ☐

3 Geben Sie an, wann Sie die Tätigkeiten aus Übung 2 ausüben.

1 *I get up at seven o'clock.*

2 ______

3 ______

4 ______

5 ______

6 ______

7 ______

READING

1 Lesen Sie den Text. Unterstreichen Sie die Präpositionen der Zeit.

2 Schreiben Sie auf, was in Ihrem Land anders ist.

We don't start work at nine o'clock, we start work at half past eight.

______

The French day

Most people start work at nine in the morning and finish work at five in the evening. But teachers and schoolchildren start work at eight and finish at five. It's a very long day in a French school. Most people don't work at weekends. Some children go to school on Saturday mornings, but they don't go to school on Wednesday afternoons. The French have a small breakfast before they go to work. They have two hours at lunchtime and they usually have a big lunch. Many people go to restaurants at midday. In the evening they have another big meal at about eight o'clock.

GRAMMAR

1 Ergänzen Sie mit der richtigen Präposition: *in*, *at* oder *on*.

1 in the morning
2 at midday
3 at the weekend
4 at night
5 in the evening
6 on Sunday
7 at 7 o'clock
8 on Monday

2 Bilden Sie Sätze mit den Zeitangaben aus Übung 1.

1 *I go to work at nine in the morning.*
2 ______
3 ______
4 ______
5 ______
6 ______
7 ______
8 ______

3 Beantworten Sie die folgenden Fragen in Bezug auf Ihre Landsleute.

1 What time do children go to school?
Children go to school at half past seven in the morning
2 What time do teachers start and finish work?
They start work at quarter to eight in the morning and finish work at one o'clock in the afternoon
3 When do most people finish work?
Most people finish work between four at five in the afternoon.
4 What time do people have their lunch?
People have their lunch at twelve o'clock.

SOUNDS

1 Hören Sie sich die Fragen an. Unterstreichen Sie die betonten Wörter.

1 Do you work at the weekend?
2 Do people work on Sunday mornings?
3 Do they have lunch at home?
4 Do we finish work at five today?
5 Do you have a siesta in the afternoon?

Hören Sie noch einmal zu und wiederholen Sie.

2 Unterstreichen Sie jeweils das Wort, das einen anderen Vokallaut hat.

1 no don't home work most
2 son clock some much Monday
3 night time five write girl
4 teacher three breakfast people week

Hören Sie zu und kontrollieren Sie. Sprechen Sie die Wörter laut.

3 Hören Sie zu und schreiben Sie die Uhrzeiten auf.

1 *3.30*
2 ______
3 ______
4 ______
5 ______
6 ______
7 ______
8 ______
9 ______
10 ______

WRITING

Schauen Sie sich noch einmal den Text im Abschnitt READING an. Beschreiben Sie in ein paar Sätzen, was Sie im Urlaub tun. Inwiefern unterscheidet sich Ihr Urlaub von Ihrem Arbeitsalltag?

When I'm on holiday I get up at ten o'clock.

8 Home

VOCABULARY

1 Schreiben Sie möglichst viele Wörter auf, die zu diesen beiden Kategorien gehören.

Furniture: ______________________________

Electrical equipment: ______________________

2 Listen Sie fünf nützliche Haushaltsgegenstände auf. Wo befinden sich diese Gegenstände?

telephone: There is a telephone on the table in the hall next to the door.

1 ______________________________
2 ______________________________
3 ______________________________
4 ______________________________
5 ______________________________

3 Listen Sie die Zimmer auf, die es bei Ihnen zu Hause gibt.

____
____

4 Erzählen Sie, was Sie in diesen Zimmern tun.

____
____
____
____
____

GRAMMAR

1 Ergänzen Sie die Sätze mit *is* oder *are*.

1 There __________ four bedrooms.
2 There __________ a sitting room with a sofa.
3 There __________ some chairs next to the table.
4 There __________ (not) any books.
5 __________ there any curtains in the bedroom?
6 There __________ (not) a video.
7 __________ there a dishwasher?
8 There __________ a car in the garage.

2 Ergänzen Sie die Sätze mit *some* oder *any.*

1 There aren't __________ armchairs in the bedrooms.
2 There are __________ books on the shelf.
3 There are __________ shutters in the room upstairs.
4 Are there __________ plants in the sitting room?
5 He hasn't got __________ curtains in his room.
6 They have __________ videos in the cupboard.

LISTENING

1 Hören Sie zu, wie drei Personen ihr Lieblingszimmer beschreiben. Welches Zimmer wird jeweils beschrieben?

Speaker 1: ______________
Speaker 2: ______________
Speaker 3: ______________

2 Hören Sie noch einmal zu und ergänzen Sie die Sätze.

Room 1

1 My favourite room is a small __________.
2 It is __________ next to the __________.
3 There are __________ on two walls of the room.
4 In front of the __________ is a desk with my __________.
5 There is a big __________ on the wall next to a very old __________.

Room 2

1 My favourite room is a big __________ at the back of the house.
2 There is a __________ with a view of the __________.
3 There is a comfortable __________ in front of the __________.
4 There are some pretty green __________ and an old __________.
5 The __________ and __________ are on a cupboard near the fire.

Room 3

1 I like my __________ best of all.
2 It's __________ at the front of the house.
3 There's a __________ and a small table with a __________.
4 There's a __________ next to the door.
5 There are some __________ on the table near the window.

SOUNDS

1 Wie spricht man das a in diesen Wörtern aus? Hören Sie zu und teilen Sie die Wörter in zwei Gruppen ein.

armchair bath bookcase carpet game garden large plane plant radio table washbasin

/ɑː/ *armchair* __________

/eɪ/ *bookcase* __________

2 Hören Sie zu und wiederholen Sie diese Wörter mit sh und ch.

/ʃ/ shutters shower dishwasher washbasin possession shirt

/tʃ/ kitchen chair furniture watch coach check lunch

WRITING AND READING

1 Wo befinden sich diese Gegenstände und Zimmer in Ihrem Hause? Bilden Sie Sätze.

bathroom radio bed telephone bookcase plants mirror cooker garage

The bathroom is upstairs next to my bedroom.

2 Mr & Mrs Edmunds möchten einen Haustausch machen mit einer Familie im Ausland. Lesen Sie die Beschreibung ihres Hauses in der Haustausch-Broschüre.

Where do Mr and Mrs Edmunds want to go for their holiday?

3 Sind die folgenden Sätze richtig oder falsch?

1 Mr and Mrs Edmunds have got two children.
2 They've got a house near Cambridge.
3 There is a small garden at the front of the house.
4 Their holiday is in August.
5 There isn't a garage.

Mr and Mrs G Edmunds
The Old Mill
Burwell
Cambridgeshire
Telephone: 01223 639 487

Holiday dates: 1st July to 21st July
Exchange with a house with a garden suitable for a family of five people (two adults and three small children) in Italy.

Our house is in a pretty village near Cambridge. It is in a beautiful place next to a river. It is very quiet and safe for children. The house is suitable for five people. It is quite big and there is a garden at the back. There are three bedrooms, a bathroom and a toilet upstairs. Downstairs there is a sitting room with a fire, two armchairs and a sofa. There are carpets in all the bedrooms and in the sitting room. The kitchen is at the back of the house and there is a door to the garden.

There is a dishwasher, a cooker, a washing machine and a fridge in the kitchen. There is a downstairs toilet and shower. Next to the kitchen is a small dining room. There are two telephones, a television and stereo equipment in the house. There is no garage.

4 Beschreiben Sie Ihr Haus/Ihre Wohnung für eine Haustausch-Broschüre.

9 How do you relax?

VOCABULARY

1 Suchen Sie 21 Verben in diesem Rätsel. Die Wörter können in zwei Richtungen gelesen werden (→) und (↓).

R	E	L	A	X	L	I	V	E
E	W	A	T	C	H	G	E	T
A	A	H	D	R	I	N	K	F
D	S	A	M	A	K	E	S	I
L	H	V	P	L	A	Y	T	N
E	W	E	C	L	D	O	A	I
A	O	S	O	I	G	O	R	S
R	R	E	M	K	E	A	T	H
N	K	E	E	E	S	I	N	G

2 Ergänzen Sie die Sätze mit Verben aus dem Rätsel.

1 I __________ a sauna on Wednesday evenings.
2 I __________ sport on television on Saturday afternoons.
3 I __________ the Sunday lunch for the family.
4 I __________ a sandwich and __________ mineral water for lunch.
5 I __________ the guitar in a rock band with friends.
6 I __________ Spanish at evening classes.

GRAMMAR

1 Schreiben Sie die Sätze aus VOCABULARY Übung 2 in der dritten Person Singular (der dritten Person Einzahl) noch einmal neu.

1 ______________________________
2 ______________________________
3 ______________________________
4 ______________________________
5 ______________________________
6 ______________________________

2 Ergänzen Sie die Fragen mit einem passenden Fragewort.

1 Where do you live?
2 How do you relax?
3 Who do you live with?
4 What do you do on Sundays?
5 When do you start work?

3 Beantworten Sie die Fragen in Übung 2.

1 I live in Fellbach.
2 I listen to music, exp. U2, Sting.
3 I live with my husband.
4 On Sundays relax I.
5 I start my work at eight 'o clock.

4 Was machen Sie zu den folgenden Tageszeiten?

1 at lunchtime?
____
2 on Sunday mornings?
____
3 on weekday evenings?
____
4 on Saturday evenings?
____

READING

1 Lesen Sie den Text. Erzählt hier ein Mann oder eine Frau?

____

2 Suchen Sie vier Tätigkeiten, die der Mann allein macht. Bilden Sie Sätze in der dritten Person Singular.

____
____
____
____

3 Suchen Sie drei Tätigkeiten, die seine Frau allein macht. Bilden Sie Sätze in der dritten Person Singular.

____

____

____

4 Unterstreichen Sie, was sie gemeinsam machen.

On weekdays my wife comes home at 6.30 and I come home at 7. We have a drink and then I make dinner. We sit and have dinner in front of the television. On Tuesday evenings we go to the cinema with friends and then we have a drink in a bar in town. On Wednesday evenings my wife goes to language classes and then she goes to a friend's house for dinner. I watch the sport on television when she isn't there.

At the weekend we get up at midday. On Saturday afternoon we go to the supermarket for things for the week. After that I go running or I read. In the evening we go to a restaurant with friends or to a nightclub. On Sundays we go to my wife's parents' house in the country. In the evening I watch television and my wife works on her computer. ●

LISTENING

1 Hören Sie sich zwei Frauen an. Machen Sie ein Häkchen neben die Dinge, die sie jeweils allein machen.

	Woman 1	**Woman 2**
reads the newspaper		
has a cup of tea		
makes dinner		
goes to a friend's house		
has a language class		
has dinner with a friend		
goes running		
goes to a jazz club		
works on her computer		

2 Hören Sie noch einmal zu. Welches ist die Ehefrau des Erzählers im Text im Abschnitt READING?

SOUNDS

1 Hören Sie zu und unterstreichen Sie jeweils das Wort, das eine anders klingende Endung hat.

1 does goes gets plays
2 eats has likes drinks
3 watches makes finishes relaxes
4 sees reads lives speaks

Hören Sie zu und kontrollieren Sie. Sprechen Sie die Wörter laut.

2 Hören Sie sich die Sätze an. Die unterstrichenen Laute werden zusammen gesprochen.

1 We get up at eight o'clock.
2 I get a video.
3 I watch it at night.
4 He learns a language.
5 She gets up for work.
6 He lives at home.

Hören Sie noch einmal zu und wiederholen Sie.

WRITING

Was unternehmen Sie mit Ihren Freunden in Ihrer Freizeit? Schreiben Sie vier oder fünf Sätze.

____

____

____

____

____

____

____

____

10 Do you like jazz?

SOUNDS

1 Wie viele Silben haben diese Wörter? Ordnen Sie sie in die richtige Liste ein. Unterstreichen Sie die betonten Silben.

football computer magazine unemployed
afternoon country singer cinema classical
tennis programme skating

Two syllables ______________________

____

Three syllables ______________________

____

Hören Sie zu und wiederholen Sie.

2 Hören Sie zu und wiederholen Sie diese Fragen.

1 Who's your favourite writer?
2 What type of films do you like?
3 What about you?
4 What Chinese restaurant do you go to?
5 Where do you go dancing?

VOCABULARY

1 Schreiben Sie Substantive (Hauptwörter) auf, die Sie mit diesen Verben in Verbindung bringen.

play ______________________
watch ______________________
listen to ______________________

2 Bilden Sie Sätze mit den Wörtern aus Übung 1.

____
____
____
____
____

READING

Bauen Sie die Fragen in das Gespräch ein.

A (1)
B I love tennis. I play most afternoons. (2)
A I don't like playing it very much. I only watch it on TV.
B (3)
A I like Pete Sampras.
B Yeah, he's great! (4)
A I like swimming, running and skiing in the winter. (5)
B No, I don't. But I like skating.

a What other sports do you like?
b Do you go skiing?
c What's your favourite sport?
d What about you?
e Who's your favourite player?

GRAMMAR

1 Ergänzen Sie die Aufstellung mit den Objektpronomen.

Subject	Object
I	*me*
you	______
he	______
she	______
it	______
we	______
they	______

2 Ersetzen Sie die unterstrichenen Wörter durch Objektpronomen aus der Aufstellung in Übung 1.

I like Italian films very much.
I like them very much.

1 I love modern jazz.
______
2 I don't like westerns.
______
3 I don't like classical music.
______
4 I like Emma Thompson very much.
______
5 I hate computer games.
______
6 I really like my uncle.
______

3 Bringen Sie die Wörter in die richtige Reihenfolge, um Sätze zu bilden.

1 you music do like classical?
______
2 of do type music like you what?
______
3 skiing at like not I do all.
______
4 like to cinema do the going you?
______
5 it not much like do I very.
______

4 Erzählen Sie, was Sie gerne bzw. nicht gerne machen. Verwenden Sie dabei die folgenden Verben.

play watch listen to eat drink go

jazz *I like listening to jazz.*
1 Chinese food ______
2 television ______
3 the cinema ______
4 computer games ______
5 tea ______

LISTENING

1 Sie hören zwei Gespräche. Wo finden die Gespräche jeweils statt?

a in an art gallery
b at a night club
c at a concert
d at a restaurant

2 Hören Sie noch einmal zu. Für was interessieren sich der Mann und die Frau? Machen Sie ein Häkchen im entsprechenden Kästchen.

	Man	Woman
modern art	☐	☐
classical art	☐	☐
reggae	☐	☐
classical music	☐	☐
dancing	☐	☐

WRITING

1 Beschreiben Sie drei Sachen, die Sie sehr gerne mögen sowie drei Sachen, die Sie überhaupt nicht gerne mögen.

______

2 Schreiben Sie ein Gespräch passend zu einer der zwei verbleibenden Situationen aus LISTENING Übung 1.

______

11 A day in my life

VOCABULARY AND GRAMMAR

1 Unterstreichen Sie die Adjektive. früh

late (r) usually punctual often early sometimes on time never always

2 Ergänzen Sie diese Sätze mit Wörtern aus Übung 1. Bilden Sie die Sätze aus Ihrer Sicht.

1 I __________ get to work on time.
2 I usually get up __________.
3 I __________ have a big breakfast.
4 I __________ arrive a few minutes late for my English class.
5 I always arrive __________ for an important meeting.
6 I __________ do the housework at weekends.

3 Schreiben Sie fünf Tätigkeiten auf, die Sie regelmäßig machen.

get up
____
____
____

4 Schreiben Sie in fünf Sätzen, um wieviel Uhr und wie oft Sie die fünf Tätigkeiten in Übung 3 machen.

I usually get up at seven o'clock in the morning.
1 __________
2 __________
3 __________
4 __________
5 __________

SOUNDS

1 Sprechen Sie die Uhrzeiten laut.

6 o'clock 3.15 4.30 2.10 6.45 9.50 10.05 7.20

Hören Sie zu und kontrollieren Sie.

2 Klingen die Leute glücklich oder unglücklich?

1 I always arrive on time.
2 I never go out to dinner.
3 He always gets here late.
4 She never cooks the lunch.
5 They never see their parents.
6 I always do the washing up.

Hören Sie noch einmal zu und unterstreichen Sie die betonten Wörter.

3 Führen Sie die Sätze in Übung 2 mit einigen Wörtern oder einem weiteren Satz fort.

1 *I always arrive on time for an important meeting.*
or *I always arrive on time. I don't like arriving late.*
2 __________
3 __________
4 __________
5 __________
6 __________

LISTENING

1 Schreiben Sie Wörter auf, die Sie mit diesen Berufen in Verbindung bringen.

taxi *driver drive*
teacher __________
chef __________
musician __________

2 Wer hat die folgenden Arbeitszeiten? Welche Arbeitszeit passt zu welchem Beruf in Übung 1? Schreiben Sie zu jedem Beruf einen Satz.

He/she works from seven o'clock in the morning to two o'clock in the afternoon.

a from 9.00 am to 4.30 pm
____
____

b from 8.15 pm to 2.00 am

____

____

c from 10 am to 2.15 pm and from 6.45 pm to 11.00 pm

____

____

d from 8.00 pm to 6.15 am

____

____

3 Hören Sie sich das Gespräch über den Ablauf des Arbeitstages an. Welchen Beruf aus Übung 1 üben diese Leute jeweils aus?

Speaker 1 ____________

Speaker 2 ____________

4 Hören Sie noch einmal zu. Welcher Satz passt zu welcher Person? Zwei Sätze bleiben übrig.

1 On the nights we play I have a snack at home at 7 o'clock.
2 I leave the house at 9.40.
3 I prepare my lessons and correct pupils' work in the evenings.
4 We usually start playing at 9.00 but I always get to the club at 8.15 to get things ready.
5 My wife works in the mornings and she is usually at the house when I get home.
6 We usually play for an hour and a half, then we have a break.
7 We always have a snack and a drink.
8 I don't go to work on Sundays and Mondays.
9 I get the bus at 8.30 and get to school at 9.50.
10 I get up at 8.00 most mornings and have a shower and a big breakfast with my wife.

5 Welcher Beruf in Übung 1 wird von den zwei übrig gebliebenen Sätzen beschrieben?

Write three more sentences for this job.

____

____

____

____

____

6 Ergänzen Sie die Sätze mit den angegebenen Verben.

get go leave get up have work read

I (1) ________ at 8 o'clock most mornings and (2) ________ a shower and a big breakfast with my wife. My wife (3) ________ for work at 8.45 and I relax and (4) ________ the newspaper for half an hour. I (5) ________ the house at 9.40 and walk to work. I (6) ________ lunch at the restaurant at 2 o'clock and then I walk home. My wife (7) ________ in the mornings and she is usually at the house when I (8) ________ home. In the afternoon I relax at home or go out to the park with my wife. At six o'clock I (9) ________ back to work and I (10) ________ home at 11 o'clock. I don't go to work on Sundays and Mondays.

WRITING

1 Fassen Sie den Tagesablauf des Musikers zusammen. Verwenden Sie dabei die dritte Person Singular.

____

____

____

____

____

____

____

____

____

____

2 Bilden Sie Sätze über die folgenden Situationen. Verwenden Sie dabei die Wörter aus VOCABULARY AND GRAMMAR Übung 1.

dentist work dinner party theatre English class

I always arrive early for an appointment with the dentist.

____

____

____

12 How do you get to work?

VOCABULARY

Schauen Sie sich die Bilder an. Schreiben Sie Wörter und Redewendungen auf, die diese Verkehrsmittel beschreiben.

A ______________________________

____

B ______________________________

____

C ______________________________

____

A

B

C

READING

1 Lesen Sie den Text. Zu welchem Bild passt der Text?

2 Unterstreichen Sie die Nachteile dieses Verkehrsmittels.

3 Was ist der einzige im Text erwähnte Vorteil dieses Verkehrsmittels?

4 Schauen Sie sich die Wortliste in VOCABULARY an. Wie viele Wörter erscheinen im Text wieder?

In Pakistan most people travel by bus to get from one town to another. In the less populated parts of the country many journeys take a day and there is a bus only once or twice a week. It is a dangerous means of transport and the buses sometimes break down. The roads are often in bad condition and the journeys are very slow and uncomfortable. It is a good idea to take food and drink because there are not always restaurants or shops on the route. The buses are usually very crowded with whole families travelling together. Many people sit on the roof where it is very hot in the summer and cold in winter. The only advantage of this means of transport is the cost. It is very cheap. But you only pay for what you get!

GRAMMAR

1 Schreiben Sie *a* oder *an* vor diese Wörter. Schreiben Sie die Mehrzahlform dieser Wörter auf.

_an_ appointment _appointments_

1 _____ bus __________

2 _____ coach __________

3 _____ ferry __________

4 _____ airport __________

5 _____ house __________

6 _____ office __________

7 _____ delay __________

8 _____ hour __________

2 Ergänzen Sie die Sätze mit *a*, *an* oder *the*. Falls kein Artikel notwendig ist, machen Sie einen Strich.

1 _____ number eighteen bus stops in _____ centre of town.

2 I go to _____ work by bus.

3 He works eight hours _____ day.

4 She lives and works in _____ Milan.

5 Helen is _____ secretary.

6 She works at _____ Continental tourist office near Victoria Station.

7 He takes _____ taxi twice _____ week.

8 _____ plane to Chicago leaves at seven.

9 I stay at _____ home on Thursdays.

10 She always goes to _____ office by _____ bicycle.

3 Bilden Sie passende Fragen zu diesen Antworten.

1 ______________________________

It takes about an hour.

2 ______________________________

I go by car.

3 ______________________________

No, I only go twice a month.

4 ______________________________

Fifty pence.

5 ______________________________

It's about thirty miles.

SOUNDS

1 Hören Sie zu und unterstreichen Sie die Wortverbindungen.

1 It's about eighty miles.

2 The office is near the station.

3 It's the age of the train.

4 It's quite expensive.

5 People sit on the roof.

Hören Sie noch einmal zu und wiederholen Sie.

2 Verbinden Sie die Wörter mit dem gleichen Vokalklang.

slow	ride
train	live
bus	coach
drive	long
stop	plane
quick	month

Hören Sie zu und kontrollieren Sie Ihre Antworten.

WRITING

1 Lesen Sie den Text im Abschnitt READING noch einmal. Sind Sie auch der Meinung, '*now is the age of the train*'? Wenn nicht, dann ergänzen Sie den folgenden Satz mit einem anderen Wort. Begründen Sie Ihre Meinung in ein paar Zeilen.

It's the age of the __________.

2 Schreiben Sie jeweils ein paar Zeilen zu diesen Verkehrsmitteln in Bezug auf Ihr Land.

taxis

trains

buses and coaches

13 Can you swim?

VOCABULARY AND GRAMMAR

1 Füllen Sie das Kreuzworträtsel aus. Sie dürfen dabei Ihr *Student's Book* verwenden.

Across

3 You do this in water.
6 You can do this in a kitchen.
8 You can't eat water, you _____ it.
9 Infinitive of *am*.
12 *Does* in the 1st person.
13 What you do on a horse.
17 You need a book or a magazine to do this.
18 To be first in a race you _____.
19 Pigs can't do this, nor can chickens, but planes can.

Down

1 You can't do it in the summer.
2 To have something in your hand.
4 To go on foot.
5 They _____ their friends at the club on Sundays.
7 To make a sweater.
10 Don't stop.
11 What you do with a car.
14 To make a picture.
15 You _____ a meal.
16 Can you _____ a musical instrument?
17 I can't _____ 100 metres in 15 seconds.

2 Ergänzen Sie die Sätze mit *can* oder *can't*.

1 I __________ do crosswords at all.
2 He __________ knit quite well.
3 They __________ speak English very well, but they __________ write it.
4 She __________ swim, but not very fast.
5 I __________ dance quite well, but I __________ cook at all.

3 Schreiben Sie fünf Sätze über das, was Sie tun können (*can do*) bzw. nicht tun können (*can't do*). Verwenden Sie dabei die Ausdrücke *very well*, *quite well* sowie *not at all*.

1 ______________________________
2 ______________________________
3 ______________________________
4 ______________________________
5 ______________________________

4 Schreiben Sie passende Fragen oder Sätze zu den Antworten.

1 ______________________________
Yes, I can.
2 ______________________________
Nor can I.
3 ______________________________
No, I can't.
4 ______________________________
So can I.

SOUNDS

1 Hören Sie zu und unterstreichen Sie die Buchstaben, die nicht ausgesprochen werden.

cupboard daylight foreign hour knit listen night often walk write

Hören Sie noch einmal zu und wiederholen Sie.

2 Hören Sie zu und machen Sie ein Häkchen, wenn der unterstrichene Laut /æ/ ausgesprochen wird oder ein Kreuzchen, wenn der unterstrichene Laut /ə/ ausgesprochen wird.

1 I can speak English fluently.
2 Can you drive a car?
3 I can cook quite well.
4 So can I.
5 I can play the guitar.
6 Yes, I can!

Hören Sie zu und wiederholen Sie.

READING AND WRITING

1 Wie heißen die abgebildeten Gegenstände? Schreiben Sie die Wörter darunter.

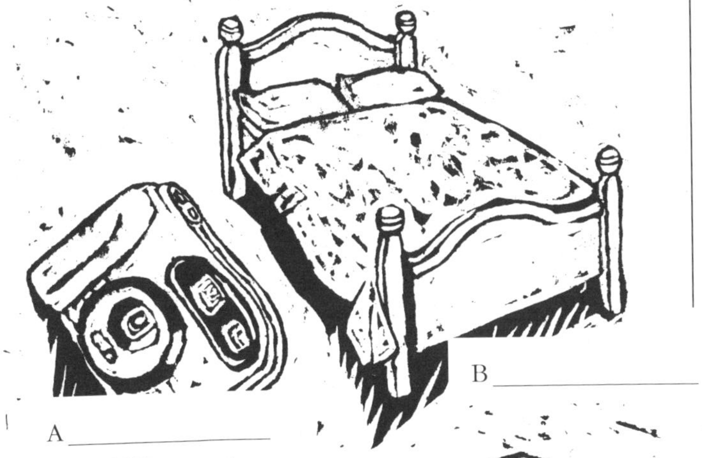

A ________________ B ________________

C ________________ D ________________ E ________________ F ________________

2 Welche Beschreibung passt zu welchem Gegenstand?

1 This is a machine. It can wash plates. It is usually in the kitchen.
2 It is often upstairs in a house. You can sleep in it or just lie on it.
3 This is often in the sitting room. You can put it on and watch a programme. You can also use it to watch a video.
4 This thing can take pictures. It is not very big and you can carry it in your bag.
5 It is often in the sitting room. It is hot. You can sit in front of it when you are cold.
6 If you look in it you can see yourself. It can be on a wall in any room of the house. There is always one in the bathroom.

3 Machen Sie einen Kreis um alle Verben, die in den Beschreibungen in Übung 2 erscheinen. Kontrollieren Sie, ob Sie die richtige Bedeutung dieser Verben kennen.

4 Unterstreichen Sie die Wörter, die beschreiben, wo sich die Gegenstände normalerweise befinden.

5 Formulieren Sie ähnliche Beschreibungen für die folgenden Gegenstände.

a radio
____
____

a car
____
____

a mobile phone
____
____

14 How do I get to Queen Street?

VOCABULARY

1 Unterstreichen Sie alle Verben in dem Kästchen.

kleider

meal suncream stamps send lamp clothes
account medicine eat menu cassette buy
magazine platform aspirin dinner money
newspaper sweets ticket traveller's cheques
letters take out train envelopes change

2 Welche Wörter aus dem Kästchen passen zu welchem Ort? Einige Wörter bleiben übrig.

post office stamps, send, buy, envelopes
newsagent's letters, newspaper
chemist's suncream, aspirin, buy, medicine
bank change, send, account
station train, ticket, platform
restaurant meal, sweets, dinner

3 Schreiben Sie zu jedem Ort in Übung 2 einen Satz.

You can buy stamps in a post office.

1 ______
2 ______
3 ______
4 ______
5 ______
6 ______

GRAMMAR AND READING

1 Lesen Sie die Beschreibung von Hereford-Stadtmitte. Kontrollieren Sie, ob Sie alle unterstrichenen Wörter richtig verstanden haben.

2 Unterstreichen Sie alle Präpositionen des Ortes.

3 Markieren Sie die folgenden Gebäude auf dem Plan.

museum shopping mall bank
tourist information centre chemist's post office
indoor market park hotel

Hereford is a small market town in the west of England. The High Street is very short with a big square at the end of it called High Town. There are a lot of attractive shops in High Town and there are no cars. You can visit the beautiful Old House which is a museum in the middle of High Town. There is a post office behind the Old House opposite the bookshop. There is a bank with a cash machine opposite the library in Broad Street. There is an indoor food market in High Town between Gromond Street and Widemarsh Street. Behind the market is a small shopping mall called Maylord Orchards. There is a big chemist's shop in the High Street opposite the newsagent's. At the end of Church Street there is a small park and the cathedral. In Broad Street, on the same side of the road as the library, is a very good hotel and restaurant called The Green Dragon.
The tourist information office is on the corner of Broad Street and King Street opposite the library.
Wednesday is market day and the town is very busy. There is a big market out of the town centre where you can buy all sorts of things. There is also a cattle market where they sell cows, sheep and pigs.

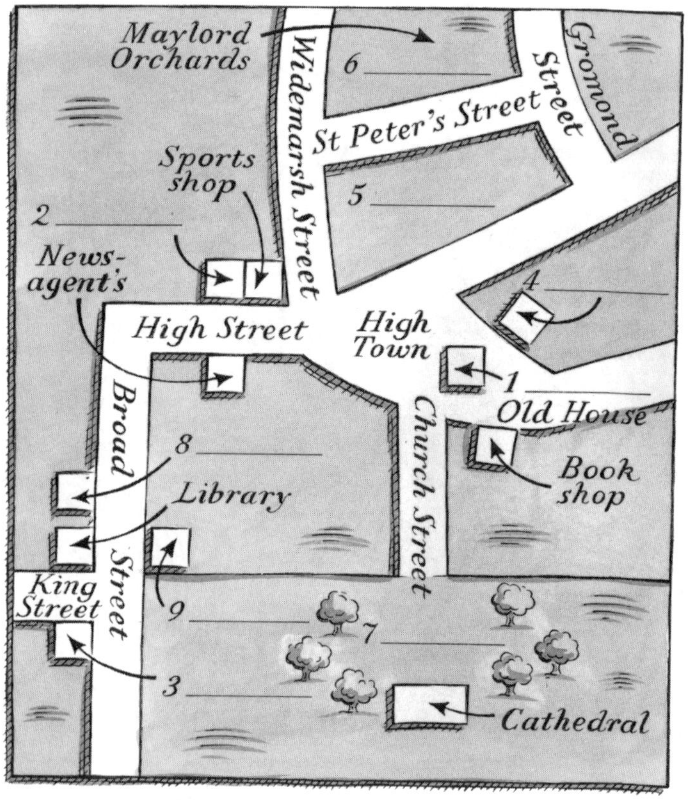

4 Schauen Sie sich den Stadtplan an. Ergänzen Sie die Sätze mit einer Präposition des Ortes.

1 The tourist information centre is __________ the library.

2 The museum is in High Town __________ the post office and the bookshop.

3 The newsagent's is __________ the chemist's.

4 The library is __________ Broad Street and King Street.

5 The shopping mall is __________ the indoor market.

6 The sports shop is __________ the chemist's and __________ the newsagent's.

LISTENING

1 Schauen Sie sich den Plan an. Sie hören nun drei Gespräche im Fremdenverkehrsbüro. Was möchten diese Leute?

Conversation 1 ____________________

Conversation 2 ____________________

Conversation 3 ____________________

2 Hören Sie sich die Gespräche Nr. 1 und Nr. 2 noch einmal an und ergänzen Sie jeweils die Wegbeschreibung.

Conversation 1

1 Go __________ Broad Street.

2 Turn __________ into the High Street, then __________ __________ into High Town.

3 The post office is __________ the bookshop, __________ the Old House.

Conversation 2

1 Walk __________ Broad Street.

2 The chemist's is __________ the newsagent's.

3 It's __________ __________ __________ of a sports shop.

3 Hören Sie sich das Gespräch Nr. 3 noch einmal an und unterstreichen Sie alles im Text, was nicht mit dem Gespräch übereinstimmt.

A Hello, Peter. How are you?
B Fine, thanks. Why are you here in town?
A I'm with my husband. We are looking for a nice place to have a meal. Can you tell me where there is a good French restaurant?
B Yes. There's a restaurant called Pasta in Widemarsh Street. It has a good reputation.
A How can I get to Widemarsh Street from here? Is it far?
B No. About twenty minutes' walk. Go down Broad Street. Turn right into the High Street, then turn left into Widemarsh Street. Go along there for about ten metres and the restaurant is on the right, next to the baker's. There's an Italian restaurant on the same side of the road.
A Thanks. Bye.

WRITING

1 Ergänzen Sie den Dialog.

A ____________________
B At the vegetable market.
A ____________________
B No, it's very near. It's only about five minutes' walk from here.
A ____________________
B Yes. You go along the High Street until you get to the square. The entrance to the market is on your left next to a big shoe shop.
A ____________________
B The vegetable shops are inside the market on the left.
A ____________________
B Yes. There are two florist's at the opposite end of the market hall.
A ____________________

2 Wählen Sie drei Ziele in Ihrem Wohnort aus. Schreiben Sie jeweils eine Wegbeschreibung von Ihrem Haus bis dorthin.

____
____
____
____
____

15 *What's happening?*

GRAMMAR

1 Schreiben Sie das Partizip Präsens dieser Verben auf.

enjoy *enjoying*
stay ________
pass ________
have ________
live ________
learn ________
shop ________
sit ________
fly ________
travel ________
take ________
lie ________
write ________

2 Ergänzen Sie die Sätze mit Verben in der Verlaufsform Präsens (Verlaufsform Gegenwart). Wählen Sie die Verben aus der Liste in Übung 1.

1 We ____________ in a very cheap hotel on the coast.
2 She ____________ on the beach in the sun.
3 They ____________ dinner outside.
4 We ____________ at 10,000 metres.
5 I hope you ____________ the flight.

3 Bilden Sie sechs Sätze in der Verlaufsform Präsens. Verwenden Sie dabei Verben aus der Liste in Übung 1.

1 ________________________________
2 ________________________________
3 ________________________________
4 ________________________________
5 ________________________________
6 ________________________________

SOUNDS

1 Wie viele Silben haben die folgenden Wörter? Ordnen Sie die Wörter jeweils in die richtige Liste ein. Unterstreichen Sie die betonten Silben.

beautiful attractive ugly industrial lively
modern mountains wonderful boring

Two syllables ________________________
____
Three syllables ________________________
____
Four syllables ________________________
____

Hören Sie zu und kontrollieren Sie. Sprechen Sie die Wörter laut.

2 Hören Sie zu und unterstreichen Sie die betonten Wörter.

1 We're having a wonderful time.
2 I'm not enjoying the flight.
3 She's learning to swim.
4 They're staying at an expensive hotel.
5 He's travelling for his job.
6 I'm writing this on the beach.

Hören Sie zu und wiederholen Sie.

VOCABULARY

Schreiben Sie das Gegenteil zu diesen Adjektiven auf. Sie dürfen dabei ein Wörterbuch verwenden.

beautiful *ugly*
east ________
interesting ________
old-fashioned ________
north ________
cold ________
dark ________
quiet ________

LISTENING

1 Schauen Sie sich die Fotos an. Welche Wörter beschreiben die abgebildeten Szenen?

chalet modern sea old coast skiing industrial mountains river town snow port cold holiday

2 Beschreiben Sie jedes Foto mit ein paar Wörtern oder Ausdrücken.

Picture A ______________________

Picture B ______________________

Picture C ______________________

3 Sie hören zwei Telefongespräche. Von welchem der abgebildeten Orte aus wird jeweils telefoniert?

Conversation 1 ______________________

Conversation 2 ______________________

4 Hören Sie sich die Gespräche noch einmal an. Sind diese Sätze richtig oder falsch?

Conversation 1

1 Anna is phoning her husband.
2 She's staying in a hotel outside the city.
3 She's having a wonderful time.
4 It's raining at the moment.

Conversation 2

1 Stephie is phoning her father.
2 She's staying in a hotel in the mountains.
3 She's having a holiday with her parents.
4 Her parents are visiting the town at the moment.

READING AND WRITING

1 Lesen Sie die Beschreibung von Monaco. Unterstreichen Sie die Ausdrücke, die beschreiben, wo Monaco liegt.

2 Was lockt die Besucher nach Monaco? Suchen Sie fünf Gründe.

MONACO is the world's second smallest country after the Vatican. There are only 30,000 inhabitants. It is on the Mediterranean coast in the south-east of France near Italy. Monaco-Ville is the capital. Many tourists visit Monaco because of its beautiful location between the mountains and the sea and also because of its pleasant climate. Others go there for the gambling casinos or to see the famous Formula 1 motor race. Many rich people from different countries live in Monaco because there are no taxes.

3 Beschreiben Sie in ein paar Sätzen eine Ihnen bekannte Großstadt. Erzählen Sie, warum diese Stadt für Sie interessant ist.

____

____

____

____

____

____

A

B

C

16 Who was your first friend?

VOCABULARY AND READING

1 **Lesen Sie die Texte und entscheiden Sie, zu welchem Text diese Sätze gehören.**

a My first holiday without my parents was in Greece.

b It was the worst holiday I can remember.

c She was my first girlfriend.

d My first pet was a dog.

2 **Wer oder was in den Texten wird von diesen Wörtern und Ausdrücken beschrieben?**

noisy shy horrid exciting dark wonderful not well-behaved naughty attractive hot bad-tempered terrible not obedient

■ (1) **His name was Toby.** He was a small, brown dog with a long tail. He was noisy and often quite naughty and he wasn't at all obedient. But he was my best friend when I was a child and we were always together.

■ (2) **I was seventeen years old.** It was very exciting because it was the first time I was not with my parents. There were four of us. We were all good friends from the same school. It was in August and we were there for two weeks. I remember it was very hot. It was a wonderful holiday and one of my best memories.

GRAMMAR

1 **Ergänzen Sie diese Sätze mit *was* oder *were*.**

1 She __________ late for work this morning.

2 They __________ in London last week.

3 I __________ at home yesterday.

4 We __________ at the restaurant last night.

5 You __________ with your brother yesterday.

6 The weather __________ very wet last month.

■ **She was very shy and very attractive.** She wasn't very tall and she had long, dark hair. We were at the same school but we weren't in the same class. She was good at music and art and I was good at languages and maths. We were both fourteen years old and we were always together. (3)

■ **I remember that holiday very well because it was terrible.** I was in a caravan by the sea for a week with my parents and two brothers. The weather was horrid. Every day it was cold and wet. There wasn't one sunny day during the week. Because there was nothing to do we weren't very well-behaved and our parents were bad-tempered. It was good to get back home. (4)

2 Bringen Sie die Wörter in die richtige Reihenfolge, um Fragen zu bilden.

1 were where born you?

____

2 like were you school what at?

____

3 friend at was who school your best?

____

4 at you good were what?

____

5 trouble often were school you at in?

____

3 Beantworten Sie die Fragen in Übung 2.

1 ______________________________
2 ______________________________
3 ______________________________
4 ______________________________
5 ______________________________

4 Beantworten Sie diese Fragen in Bezug auf gestern.

1 What day was it?

____

2 What was the weather like?

____

3 Where were you in the morning?

____

4 Were you alone or with other people?

____

VOCABULARY AND SOUNDS

1 Unterstreichen Sie die betonten Silben in den folgenden Wörtern.

stubborn obedient lazy cheerful horrid
untidy polite naughty disappointing

2 Was oder wen würden Sie mit den oben genannten Adjektiven beschreiben.

____
____
____
____
____

3 Hören Sie zu und wiederholen Sie die Fragen in GRAMMAR Übung 2.

LISTENING

1 Hören Sie sich das folgende Gespräch an. Nummerieren Sie die Fragen in der richtigen Reihenfolge.

a Where were you? ☐
b How was your holiday? ☐
c Were you in a good hotel? ☐
d What about the food? ☐
e What was the weather like? ☐
f Who were you with? ☐

2 Beantworten Sie die Fragen in Übung 1 in Bezug auf Ihren letzten Urlaub.

1 ______________________________
2 ______________________________
3 ______________________________
4 ______________________________
5 ______________________________
6 ______________________________

WRITING

Lesen Sie die Texte in VOCABULARY AND READING noch einmal durch. Schreiben Sie einen ähnlichen Text über eines der folgenden Themen.

your first boy/girlfriend   your first pet
your first holiday without your parents
your worst/best family holiday

____
____
____
____
____
____
____
____

17 How about some oranges?

VOCABULARY

1 Unterstreichen Sie jeweils das Wort, das nicht zu den anderen passt.

1 beef rice pork lamb chicken
2 butter cheese milk bacon yoghurt
3 potato banana apple orange grape
4 water wine juice milk oil
5 knife fork plate salt spoon
6 meat onion vegetables fruit drink

2 Schreiben Sie drei Gerichte auf, die für Ihr Land typisch sind. Listen Sie ein paar Zutaten zu jedem Gericht auf.

Knödel Kohl Schweinebraten
- dumpling with cabbage and roast pork

____
____
____

READING AND WRITING

1 Lesen Sie den Text durch. Sind die folgenden Aussagen richtig oder falsch?

1 They sometimes sit on the floor when they eat.
2 They often use chopsticks.
3 They don't use their fingers.
4 They can't drink alcohol in public.
5 Smoking is common.
6 They don't put salt on the table.
7 They eat early in the evening.
8 Restaurants are very formal.

2 Lesen Sie den Text noch einmal durch. Finden Sie heraus: Was ist ...

informal eating habits
common ______________________________
____
crowded, noisy and hot ______________________________
____
relaxed ______________________________
____

3 Sind die im Text unterstrichenen Wörter zählbar oder nicht zählbar ? Schreiben Sie C (*countable* = zählbar) oder U (*uncountable* = nicht zählbar) über jedes Wort.

4 Korrigieren Sie die falschen Aussagen in Übung 1.

1 ______________________________
2 ______________________________
3 ______________________________
4 ______________________________

Eating habits are very informal. You sit at a table or in a circle on the floor around the food. All the food is put out on different plates at the start of the meal. You take what you want. Most people eat with a spoon and a fork. You can use your fingers to make rice balls which you dip in various sauces. Chopsticks are only common with the Chinese population in Thailand. There isn't usually any salt because they use fish sauce.

Thais can eat and drink anything. There are no social taboos. Drinking alcohol is a normal social activity for men. Smoking is common among men and women.

Thais eat early in the evening. They usually have their evening meal at about six o'clock. Most traditional Thai restaurants close at about eight o'clock. So if you go early, it is crowded, noisy and hot and if you go late there is no food left! These restaurants are very relaxed. You can even take your own drink into a Thai restaurant!

GRAMMAR AND LISTENING

1 Schreiben Sie C (*countable* = zählbar) oder U (*uncountable* = nicht zählbar) hinter jedes Wort.

wine	____	apple	____	oil	____
yoghurt	____	egg	____	butter	____
onion	____	pork	____	lemon	____
milk	____	carrot	____	water	____
beef	____	bread	____	tea	____
salt	____	rice	____	soup	____
steak	____	pasta	____	cheese	____

2 Ergänzen Sie die Sätze mit *some*, *any* oder *a/an*.

1 We need __some__ mineral water. - RE
2 Let's have __some__ fruit.
3 Can I have __a__ banana, please?
4 I'm sorry. We haven't got __any__ bananas.
5 How about __some__ pasta?
6 I need __a__ cup of coffee.

3 Lesen Sie den Dialog durch. Um was für eine Situation handelt es sich?

in Restaurant – to order

4 Ergänzen Sie den Dialog mit *some*, *any* oder *a/an*.

Listen and check.

A I'd like (1) __some__ vegetable soup with bread, please ×

B I'm afraid we haven't got (2) __any__ soup today, madam. But we've got (3) __some__ potato salad. ×

A I don't like salads. I'll have (4) __a__ cheese omelette.

B Cheese omelette. And for the main course? (Hauptgericht)

A Roast chicken with boiled potatoes.

B I'm sorry, but we haven't got (5) __any__ chicken. But you can have (6) __a__ steak. And there is pasta or chips instead of boiled potatoes.

A All right. A steak and chips. Have you got (7) __any__ wine or is there only water or tea? ×

B Of course, madam. We've got (8) __a__ good Bulgarian red wine.

A Haven't you got (9) __any__ white wine?

B Yes. It's German.

A That's fine. And cheese. I'd like (10) __some__ cheese and (11) __an__ ice cream.

B Do you want (12) __any__ water?

A Yes, please. A bottle of spring water.

WRITING

1 Schauen Sie sich das Foto einer britischen Hochzeitsfeier an. Beschreiben Sie das Bild in ein paar Sätzen.

2 Beschreiben Sie eine typische Hochzeitsfeier in Ihrem Lande.

18 *I was born in England*

VOCABULARY

1 Welches Wort passt zu welcher Definition?

album award group guitar hit musician piano singer teenager

1 a very popular song or piece of music hit
2 a young person teenager
3 a collection of songs or pieces of music album
4 someone who plays an instrument piano
5 more than one musician group
6 something a singer can receive when he or she sells a lot of records award
7 most pop groups have one or more of these instruments guitar

2 Fügen Sie die passenden Satzteile zusammen. Sie dürfen dabei Ihr *Student's Book* verwenden.

1	She was born	a	in the film *The Bodyguard*.
2	He created	b	a hit with her first album.
3	She appeared	c	to sing on his own in 1984.
4	She received	d	the group *The Police* in 1978.
5	He started	e	as a teacher in Newcastle.
6	He played	f	an award for a song.
7	He worked	g	in New Jersey in 1964.
8	She had	h	the piano and the guitar.

GRAMMAR AND READING

1 Schreiben Sie das einfache Präteritum (die einfache Vergangenheit) dieser Verben auf.

appear	________	marry	________
create	________	move	________
die	________	play	________
learn	________	start	________
live	________	work	________
compose	________	finish	________

2 Ergänzen Sie diese Sätze mit einem Verb im einfachen Präteritum aus der Liste in Übung 1.

1 Sting ________ Trudy Styler in 1986.
2 Whitney Houston ________ in *The Bodyguard.*
3 As a child he ________ to play the piano and guitar.
4 As a teenager she ________ with rhythm and blues singers.
5 Sting ________ to sing on his own in 1984.
6 Sting ________ the group *The Police.*

3 Lesen Sie den Text über Mozart und ergänzen Sie ihn mit Verben im einfachen Präteritum aus der Liste in Übung 1.

Mozart was born in 1756 in Austria. As a child he (1) ________ to play the harpsichord, the violin and the piano. When he was five years old he (2) ________ writing music. He (3) ________ in public all over Europe before he was ten. He (4) ________ in Italy from 1768 to 1771. In 1771 he (5) ________ to Saltzburg and organized concerts there. In 1781 he (6) ________ to Vienna and he (7) ________ Constanze Weber, a singer. In 1786 he created his first important opera, *The Marriage of Figaro*. In the following year he (8) ________ as the official court musician to Joseph II. In 1788 he (9) ________ his three last symphonies. Mozart (10) ________ a poor man at the age of 35.

SOUNDS

1 Unterstreichen Sie jeweils das Wort, das eine anders klingende Endung hat.

1 lived opened talked played received
2 worked appeared looked liked finished
3 enjoyed died loved visited married
4 decided started wanted created watched

Hören Sie zu und kontrollieren Sie.

2 Hören Sie zu und unterstreichen Sie die betonten Wörter.

1 She was born in London.
2 He learned to play the piano.
3 She received an award.
4 They created the group *The Police*.
5 He started work as a teacher.

Hören Sie noch einmal zu und wiederholen Sie.

LISTENING

1 Kennen Sie die abgebildeten Stars? Schreiben Sie zu jedem ein paar Worte.

1 Kevin Costner ______________________________

____

2 Jodie Foster ______________________________

____

3 Elton John ______________________________

Kevin Costner
Elton John
Jodie Foster

2 Sie hören nun zwei Gespräche. Um welchen Star handelt es sich jeweils?

Conversation 1 ______________________________
Conversation 2 ______________________________

3 Hören Sie sich das erste Gespräch noch einmal an und ergänzen Sie die Sätze.

1 He ______________ in Los Angeles in 1955.
2 He ______________ business at the University of California.
3 He ______________ an Oscar for his film *Dances with Wolves*.
4 He ______________ in the film *The Bodyguard* with Whitney Houston.
5 He ______________ in *Robin Hood*.

4 Hören Sie sich das zweite Gespräch noch einmal an und machen Sie sich Notizen zu den folgenden Punkten.

when she was born ______________________________
her nationality ______________________________
where she studied ______________________________
her film career ______________________________

WRITING

1 Schreiben Sie eine Beschreibung von Jodie Foster. Verwenden Sie dabei Ihre Notizen aus LISTENING Übung 4.

____
____
____
____
____

2 Schreiben Sie einen kurzen Text über Elton John. Verwenden Sie dabei die unten stehenden Informationen.

Birth place: *Middlesex, England*
Date of birth: *1947*
As a child: *piano lessons*
Work: *pianist in the 1960s*
Hits: *between 1972 and 1980 40 hits in the USA*
Concerts: *first western star to play in Moscow*
Image: *extraordinary glasses*

____
____
____

19 What's he like?

VOCABULARY

1 Schreiben Sie Adjektive auf, mit denen man folgende persönliche Merkmale beschreiben könnte:

hair curly, dark, straight, long, fair

body build wel-built, slim, small, short, tall, medium-height

personality friendly, kind, serious

age young, old, middle-aged, elderly

2 Schauen Sie sich die Bilder an und lesen Sie die Beschreibungen dazu. Unterstreichen Sie die Aussagen, die nicht stimmen.

3 Korrigieren Sie die Beschreibungen in Übung 2. Bilden Sie Sätze.

C *She's an elderly woman with an attractive face. She's fair with very short, curly hair. She's not very tall and she's got glasses.*

A *She is about thirty-five years old. She's about one metre sixty-five. She's quite slim and very attractive. She's got long, curly hair. She's got glasses.*

B *He's middle-aged and rather good-looking. He's very tall and well-built. He's dark with short, straight hair.*

FUNCTIONS

1 Schreiben Sie passende Fragen zu diesen Antworten.

1 ______________________________
He's very nice.

2 ______________________________
She's medium-height and she's got long, fair hair.

3 ______________________________
She's one metre sixty-five.

4 ______________________________
He's fifty-two.

5 ______________________________
She looks like her mother.

6 ______________________________
She usually wears fashionable clothes.

2 Beantworten Sie diese Fragen für sich selbst.

1 ______________________________
2 ______________________________
3 ______________________________
4 ______________________________
5 ______________________________
6 ______________________________

SOUNDS

Hören Sie zu und sprechen Sie diese Wörter laut.

built kind slim time nice thin smile polite sixty child

Is the vowel sound /ɪ/ or /aɪ/? Put the words in two groups.

/ɪ/: ______________________________
/aɪ/: ______________________________

LISTENING

1 Hören Sie sich die folgenden drei Beschreibungen an. Wer wird beschrieben? Nummerieren Sie die Kästchen 1 bis 3.

a new baby ☐ a criminal ☐ a new boss ☐
an old classmate ☐ a lost child ☐

2 Hören Sie sich die erste Beschreibung noch einmal an und ergänzen Sie die Sätze.

1 He's about ________ years old.
2 He's got ________, ________ hair.
3 He's wearing a ________ sweater, ________ shorts and ________ trainers.

3 Hören Sie sich die zweite Beschreibung noch einmal an. Machen Sie ein Häkchen neben die Sätze, die das jetzige Aussehen der Frau beschreiben.

1 She's small with long, dark hair.
2 She's tall and slim.
3 She wears glasses.
4 She is very hard working.
5 She's very quiet and polite.
6 She wears very smart clothes.

4 Hören Sie sich die dritte Beschreibung noch einmal an. Machen Sie sich Notizen. Erstellen Sie eine kurze Beschreibung des Mannes.

____
____
____

WRITING

Beschreiben Sie zwei Ihrer Familienmitglieder.

____
____
____
____
____
____
____

20 A grand tour

VOCABULARY

1 Suchen Sie 15 Verben in der unregelmäßigen Vergangenheitsform in diesem Rätsel. Die Wörter können in zwei Richtungen gelesen werden (→) und (↓).

F	D	I	D	M	A	D	E
O	G	B	O	U	G	H	T
U	A	C	T	O	O	K	W
N	V	A	S	A	I	D	R
D	E	M	L	O	S	T	O
H	G	E	W	E	N	T	T
A	O	S	P	E	N	T	E
D	T	B	E	C	A	M	E

2 Ergänzen Sie die Sätze mit Wörtern aus dem Rätsel.

1 I wrote a postcard to my parents.
2 He ~~went~~ did some shopping at the supermarket.
3 They came to Florence for the weekend.
4 She ~~went~~ took a train from Florence to Rome.
5 We ~~had~~ make some new friends at the hotel.
6 I haven't got a passport now because I last it when I was on holiday.

3 Fügen Sie die passenden Satzteile zusammen.

1 She went	a at home last night.
2 They found	b to Rome for her holiday.
3 I bought	c on the beach all afternoon.
4 We stayed	d the Queen when she was in London.
5 He lay	e a cheap hotel near the station.
6 She saw	f some drinks.

GRAMMAR

1 Bringen Sie die Wörter in die richtige Reihenfolge, um Fragen zu bilden.

1 yesterday visit did a you museum?
______
2 you some the did write at postcards weekend?
______
3 did do you shopping yesterday some?
______
4 Saturday you a to restaurant go on did?
______
5 you take a week did train last?
______

2 Beantworten Sie die Fragen in Übung 1 mit einem kurzen Satz.

1 ______
2 ______
3 ______
4 ______
5 ______

3 Schreiben Sie passende Fragen zu den Antworten.

Did she go to Italy last week?
Yes, she did. She went with a friend.

1 ______
No, I didn't. I went to a restaurant.

2 ______
No, we didn't. We stayed at home.

3 ______
Yes, we did. I bought some new clothes.

4 ______
Yes, he did. He enjoyed it very much.

READING

1 Schauen Sie sich den Brief kurz an. Beantworten Sie diese Fragen.

1 Who is writing?

____

2 Who is she writing to?

____

3 Is she travelling alone?

____

2 Lesen Sie den Brief. Korrigieren Sie diese Aussagen.

1 The weather was cold in London.

____

2 She spent a week in London.

____

3 She flew to Paris.

____

4 She found a cheap hotel in the Latin Quarter.

____

5 She lost her bag in a taxi.

____

6 She went to Florence after Paris.

____

7 She stayed with her cousin in Barcelona.

____

8 She spent a day by the sea near Barcelona.

____

14th May 1997

Dear Robert,

This is our third week here in Europe and we're having a great time. The people are very friendly and the weather is good – even in Britain it was sunny and warm!

We flew to London from Montreal and we spent four days visiting the city. There's so much to see and do! Unfortunately we didn't see the Queen! Mike was very disappointed!

Then we took the Eurostar to Paris and we stayed with my cousin, Angie. We did some sightseeing and we visited the Louvre and the Eiffel Tower, of course. We had some wonderful food in small restaurants in the Latin Quarter. I lost my passport in the Metro so we went to the Canadian Embassy to get another.

After Paris we flew to Barcelona where it was very hot. We made friends with some local people in a bar and they showed us the city. We took a bus to a small town on the coast and we found a hotel with a beautiful view of the sea. We relaxed on the beach for two days before moving on to Italy where we are now. We arrived here in Florence early this morning and we're having a big breakfast before we go sightseeing.

After Florence, we are going to Rome, Athens and then Istanbul. I'll write again in two weeks' time.

Give my love to Anne and the children.

See you soon!

Diana

SOUNDS

Unterstreichen Sie jeweils das Wort, das einen anderen Vokallaut hat.

1 lose good shoes blue you
2 close won love come some
3 got was lost born what
4 write fly find give buy
5 stay have take gave made

Hören Sie zu und sprechen Sie die Wörter laut.

21 Mystery

GRAMMAR AND VOCABULARY

1 Ergänzen Sie die Liste mit dem einfachen Präteritum (der einfachen Vergangenheit) dieser Verben. Unterstreichen Sie die unregelmäßigen Verben.

encourage *encouraged*
inform ______
think ______
sell ______
marry ______
leave ______
find ______
refuse ______

2 Fügen Sie die passenden Satzteile zusammen. Sie dürfen dabei Ihr Student's Book verwenden.

1	Her mother encouraged	a	to write her mysteries.
2	She married	b	the famous writer was dead.
3	She disappeared	c	her to read.
4	The police informed	d	Colonel Archibald Christie.
5	Everyone thought	e	for 11 days.
6	She continued	f	what happened in 1962.
7	She didn't explain	g	the newspapers of her disappearance.

3 Schreiben Sie auf, was Sie gestern nicht gemacht haben.

I didn't go to the cinema.
1 ______
2 ______
3 ______
4 ______
5 ______

SOUNDS

1 Wie viele Silben haben diese Wörter? Ordnen Sie sie in die richtige Liste ein.

continue disappear divorced encourage explain famous final happen inform notice refuse successful

Two syllables ______
______
Three syllables ______
______

2 Unterstreichen Sie die betonten Silben in den Wörtern aus Übung 1.

Hören Sie zu und kontrollieren Sie. Sprechen Sie die Wörter laut.

He was born in 1564 in Stratford-on-Avon. He was the son of a Stratford businessman and went to the local grammar school. In 1582 he married Anne Hathaway. They had three children. We know that he left Stratford in about 1585. But no one knows where he went or what he did for the next five years. In September 1592 we know that he lived and worked in London as a playwright and as an actor at the Globe Theatre. He is not on the actor-list after 1603 so he probably stopped acting at this time because he was already famous for his writing.

He wrote his first play, *Henry VI*, in 1590–91. He also wrote a large number of poems. He finished his last play, *The Tempest*, in 1612. After that he left London and went back to live in Stratford. He died in 1616. His plays are very successful today.

READING

1 Lesen Sie die Biografie eines berühmten englischen Schriftstellers. Können Sie erraten, um wen es sich handelt? Unterstreichen Sie alle Verben im einfachen Präteritum.

2 Bilden Sie vollständige Fragesätze über den Schriftsteller.

1 Where/born?
Where was he born?
2 When/born?
____
3 Where/go to school?
____
4 Who/marry?
____
5 Where/work as an actor?
____
6 When/stop acting?
____
7 Why/stop acting?
____
8 When/write his first play?
____
9 Where/go in 1612?
____
10 When/die?
____

3 Welche Jahre seines Lebens stellen für uns eine Lücke in seiner Biografie dar?

____

4 Beantworten Sie die Fragen in Übung 2.

1 ______________________
2 ______________________
3 ______________________
4 ______________________
5 ______________________
6 ______________________
7 ______________________
8 ______________________
9 ______________________
10 ______________________

WRITING

1 Ergänzen Sie die Biografie von Doris Lessing, einer berühmten Schriftstellerin, mit Verben aus der Liste.

be go live receive win write

Doris Lessing ____________ born of British parents in Iran in 1919 and ____________ to live in Zimbabwe when she ____________ five. As a child she ____________ on a large farm and first ____________ to England in 1949. She ____________ her first novel, *The Grass is Singing*, in 1950. It ____________ a great success in Britain and the United States. She ____________ an award for her collection of short stories, *Five*.

2 Schreiben Sie die Biografie eines weiteren berühmten Schriftstellers anhand der angegebenen Informationen. Wissen Sie, um wen es sich handelt?

born Missouri USA 1835
ship's pilot on the Mississippi in 1857
journalist in 1862 tour of Europe 1865
The Adventures of Tom Sawyer in 1876
death 1910

____
____
____
____
____
____
____
____
____
____

22 Dates

VOCABULARY AND SOUNDS

1 Schreiben Sie die Zahlen in Worten.

4th	fourth	9th	________
5th	________	12th	________
6th	________	13th	________
8th	________	15th	________

Hören Sie zu und wiederholen Sie.

2 Bilden Sie jeweils mindestens ein Substantiv (Hauptwort) aus diesen Verben. Sie dürfen dabei ein Wörterbuch verwenden.

Verb	**Noun**
discover	________
explode	________
invent	________
land	________
paint	________
take off	________
win	________

3 Ergänzen Sie die Sätze mit einem Verb aus Übung 2.

1 Germany ________ the World Cup in 1964.
2 Fleming ________ penicillin in 1928.
3 The first atom bomb ________ in 1945.
4 Picasso ________ *Guernica* in 1937.
5 Alfred Nobel ________ dynamite in 1866.
6 The first astronauts ________ on the moon on 20th July 1969.

READING

1 Lesen Sie den Text. Wählen Sie das Bild, das am besten zum Text passt.

2 Was ist an den folgenden Tagen passiert?

12th April 1981 ________
January 1986 ________
25th April 1990 ________
May 1992 ________

The US space organisation, NASA
(National Aeronautics and Space Administration) developed and built the first space shuttle. The shuttle was the first rocket to fly into space, come back to earth and fly again. The first shuttle to fly in space was *Columbia*. It took off on the 12th April 1981. In January 1986 the shuttle *Challenger* exploded at take-off. Everyone on the shuttle died. This accident slowed down the shuttle programme for the next six years. A new shuttle, *Endeavor*, replaced *Challenger* in May 1992.
On 25th April 1990, NASA used the shuttle *Discovery* to put the Hubble Space Telescope into space at a distance of 512 kilometres from the earth. Hubble travels around the earth and sends back photos of the stars and planets.

A

B

GRAMMAR

1 Nehmen Sie aus den beiden Kästchen A und B jeweils ein Wort, um einen Zeitausdruck der Vergangenheit zu bilden. Bei Bedarf können Sie einen Artikel dazu nehmen.

A	B
in on at yesterday last ago	Friday month weekend June night week 1995 10 years evening 26th March morning

in June _______________

____

____

2 Beantworten Sie die Fragen auf zwei verschiedene Weisen.

When did you last visit a museum?

I last visited a museum in March.

I last visited a museum two months ago.

1 When did you last lose something?

____

____

2 When did you last eat an egg?

____

____

3 When did you last run 100 metres?

____

____

4 When did you last sing in the bath?

____

____

5 When did you last see a funny film?

____

____

3 Schreiben Sie vier weitere Fragen mit *when*.

1 _______________
2 _______________
3 _______________
4 _______________

4 Schreiben Sie, was Sie zu folgenden Zeiten gemacht haben ...

1 last week

____

2 three weeks ago

____

3 last night

____

4 on Saturday

____

5 yesterday morning

____

6 a few minutes ago

____

LISTENING

Hören Sie zu und ergänzen Sie den Dialog mit Ausdrücken der Zeit.

MAN By the way, do you remember Janet Finch? She was at school with us.

WOMAN Yes, of course! What about her?

MAN I met her (1) _______________ at the supermarket.

WOMAN Oh, how is she? The last time I saw her was (2) _______________.

MAN She looked very well. She lived in Italy from (3) _______________ to (4) _______________. She was a teacher in Milan.

WOMAN When did she come back to Britain?

MAN (5) _______________. She spent (6) _______________ in Coventry, then she moved to Cambridge (7) _______________.

WRITING

Beschreiben Sie vier oder fünf unvergessliche Ereignisse, die in den letzten zwei Jahren Ihres Lebens stattgefunden haben.

I went to university last September.

23 What's she wearing?

VOCABULARY

1 Füllen Sie das Kreuzworträtsel aus.

1 J	A	2 C	K	E	3 T	■	■	■	4 S
E	■	O	■	■	R	■	■	■	H
A	■	A	■	■	O	■	5 S	■	O
N	■	T	■	■	U	■	U	■	R
S	■	■	■	6 T-	S	H	I	R	T
■	■	7 B	■	■	E	■	T	■	S
8 S	H	O	E	■	R	■	■	■	■
O	■	O	■	■	9 S	K	I	R	10 T
C	■	T	■	■	■	■	■	■	I
K	■	S	■	11 B	L	O	U	S	E

Across
1 The top part of a suit.
6 A casual top for everyone (two words).
8 One on each foot.
9 Only a woman wears this.
11 A woman's shirt.

Down
1 Casual trousers.
2 You need this in winter.
3 All men and some women wear them.
4 Summer clothes.
5 Jacket and trousers the same colour.
7 Footwear for winter.
8 You put it on before your shoe.
10 Very smart round a man's neck.

2 Ordnen Sie Ihre Kleidung in die folgenden Rubriken ein.

comfortable *an old T-shirt*

warm

fashionable

smart

casual

LISTENING

1 Schauen Sie sich die abgebildeten Models an. Tragen Sie ein, was sie anhaben.

2 Hören Sie sich den Kommentar zur Modeschau an. Tragen Sie die Nummer des Kommentars in das richtige Kästchen ein.

3 Hören Sie noch einmal zu. Tragen Sie die Farbe der Kleidungsstücke ein.

4 Wählen Sie ein Model aus und beschreiben Sie die Kleidung.

5 Beschreiben Sie eine Kleiderkombination, die Sie besitzen und besonders gerne tragen.

READING AND GRAMMAR

1 Lesen Sie den Brief durch. Beantworten Sie diese Fragen.

1 Who is writing to who?

2 Where is the writer?

3 Who is Aunt Grace?

2 Unterstreichen Sie vier Verben in der Verlaufsform Präsens (Verlaufsform der Gegenwart). Unterstreichen Sie vier Verben im einfachen Präsens (in der einfachen Gegenwart).

3 Suchen Sie diese Adjektive im Brief. Wer oder was wird jeweils beschrieben?

expensive ______
wonderful ______
beautiful ______
lovely ______
interesting ______
happy ______

Dear Sarah,

I'm having a wonderful holiday here in New Zealand. I'm staying in Wellington with my Aunt Grace – she's my mother's cousin. Aunt Grace is 58 years old.

She's a small lady with short, dark hair. She's got lovely brown eyes and she wears round glasses. She smiles all the time and she talks non-stop. She is very interesting because she reads a lot. She came to live in New Zealand when she was 25. She doesn't know any of her nephews and nieces back home because she never goes to Britain. She says it's too far and too expensive and she's very happy where she is.

She's a chief gardener in a big city park, but she's having a holiday this week because I'm staying with her. Every day we visit somewhere different. The scenery is beautiful in the mountains. I'm staying here for two weeks, then I'm flying to Australia for another three weeks.

See you soon,

Love,

Pat

4 Wählen Sie die richtige Zeitform des Verbs.

1 We *stay/are staying* in an expensive hotel by the sea.
2 They *live/are living* in Milan in the winter.
3 He usually *wears/is wearing* smart clothes.
4 She *is looking/looks* for a new flat at the moment.
5 He *goes/is going* to work by car every day.
6 She *laughs/is laughing* because he said something funny.

WRITING

Beschreiben Sie sich selbst und auch das, was Sie im Moment anhaben. Verwenden Sie dabei die Verlaufsform Präsens.

I'm wearing comfortable shoes ...

24 I'm going to save money

VOCABULARY

1 Ergänzen Sie die Sätze mit diesen Verben.

save stop spend study worry invite

1 I'm going to __________ at Oxford University.
2 I'm going to __________ smoking.
3 I'm not going to __________ about my work anymore.
4 We're going to __________ money to buy a house.
5 I'm not going to __________ so much money on clothes.
6 I'm going to __________ friends for dinner on Saturday.

2 Fügen Sie die passenden zwei Satzteile zusammen.

1 They're going to travel	a to him.
2 I'm looking forward	b in a few minutes.
3 She studied	c together.
4 It's going to leave	d around the world.
5 She waved goodbye	e very hard at school.
6 They grew up	f to seeing her again.

GRAMMAR

1 Schauen Sie sich die Bilder an. Was haben diese Menschen vor?

1 __________
2 __________
3 __________
4 __________

2 Ergänzen Sie die Pläne mit passenden Gründen.

1 I'm going to change my job
because I don't enjoy it.
2 I'm going to buy a bicycle
____
3 He's going to save money
____
4 We're going to go running once a week
____
5 She's going to spend more time at home
____

3 Ergänzen Sie die Sätze mit entsprechenden Vorhaben. Verwenden Sie dabei *so*.

He is very ambitious
so he is going to find a more important job.
1 I can't swim
____
2 Jane doesn't know anyone here
____
3 They don't like living in the city centre
____
4 We don't know the USA
____
5 I'm saving a thousand pounds
____

4 Erzählen Sie in einigen Sätzen, was Sie diese Woche auf keinen Fall machen werden. Erklären Sie warum.

____
____
____
____
____
____

SOUNDS

1 Hören Sie zu. Machen Sie ein Häkchen neben die Sätze, in denen das Wort *to* /tu:/ ausgesprochen wird. Machen Sie ein Kreuzchen neben die Sätze, in denen das Wort *to* /tə/ ausgesprochen wird.

1 We're going to see a film.
2 She's going to eat at home tonight.
3 I'm going to work on my own.
4 We're going to invite friends for dinner.
5 I'm going to get fit.

Hören Sie noch einmal zu und wiederholen Sie. Beachten Sie, dass das g am Wortende von *going* stumm ist.

2 Hören Sie zu. Achten Sie darauf, wie die unterstrichenen Konsonanten einen einzigen Laut bilden und zusammen gesprochen werden.

1 she found time
2 next door
3 played together
4 went to the same school
5 spend time
6 I need to

Hören Sie noch einmal zu und wiederholen Sie.

LISTENING

1 Sie hören nun ein Gespräch über Zukunftspläne. Um was für Pläne handelt es sich?

a moving to a new home
b planning a business trip
c retirement plans

2 Hören Sie noch einmal zu. Ergänzen Sie die Sätze.

1 Chris is __________ years old.
2 He doesn't __________ for the building company any more because he is retired.
3 Betty and Chris are going on a two-month __________.
4 They're going to ____________________.
5 They're not going to __________ to the country, they're going to stay in __________.
6 They're going to move to a small __________ near the __________.

WRITING

1 Schauen Sie sich den Wochenplan dieser berufstätigen Frau an. Was für einen Beruf übt sie aus?

saleswoman magazine fashion writer
interpreter hat designer

Monday	2 pm Visit the hat exhibition at the new art and design college
Tuesday	7.15 am Eurostar to Paris 11 am Interview with Paris clothes designer
Wednesday	Editorial meeting for January edition
Thursday	Piccadilly clothes show
Friday	Finish article on hats
Saturday	Party at Pete and Jenny's
Sunday	Visit parents in Oxford

2 Schreiben Sie ein paar Sätze über Ihre Pläne für die kommende Woche.

____

____

____

3 Stellen Sie Ihren eigenen Wochenplan zusammen.

Monday	
Tuesday	
Wednesday	
Thursday	
Friday	
Saturday	
Sunday	

4 Schreiben Sie ein paar Sätze über Ihre Pläne.

____

____

____

25 *Eating out*

VOCABULARY

1 Ergänzen Sie die Sätze mit Wörtern aus der Liste.

menu taste waiter tip bill course coffee reservation starter order dessert service

a When you arrive at the restaurant a __________ shows you where to sit.
b The waiter brings you the __________ at the end of the meal.
c There is often a __________ charge but some people leave a __________ as well.
d The first course or __________ is usually something light, a salad, for example.
e After the dessert you can have a __________.
f Before you go to the restaurant, it is a good idea to make a __________.
g He brings you the __________ and leaves you to choose.
h This is followed by the main __________ and finally the __________.
i If you have wine he asks you to __________ it.
j He comes and takes your __________.

2 Die Sätze beschreiben einen Besuch in einem Restaurant. Bringen Sie die Sätze in die richtige Reihenfolge.

READING AND LISTENING

1 Schauen Sie sich die Dialoge an. Wo finden sie jeweils statt?

a in a restaurant
b in a pub
c a school canteen
d at home

Dialogue 1

A Look, there are some seats in the corner.
B You three go and sit down and I'll get the orders. What would you like?
A I'd like a gin and tonic, please.
B Would you like ice with your gin?
A Yes, please.
C And I'd like a mineral water, please. No ice.
B Would you like anything to eat?
A No, thanks.
C I'd like some crisps, please.

Dialogue 2

A Would you like some salad with your steak?
B No, thanks, but can I have some more chips, please.
A Yes, help yourself. But leave some for your sister.
B Can I get the tomato ketchup?
A Yes, it's in the fridge. Can you bring me a glass of water from the kitchen?
B Is there any mustard?
A I'm afraid there isn't any left.

2 Hören Sie sich die Dialoge an. Unterstreichen Sie alles, was nicht mit dem, was Sie hören, übereinstimmt.

3 Hören Sie noch einmal zu. Korrigieren Sie die obigen Dialoge. Schreiben Sie die Korrekturen jeweils über die von Ihnen unterstrichenen Wörter oder Ausdrücke.

FUNCTIONS

1 Wer in einem Restaurant würde die folgenden Sätze verwenden? Der Ober oder der Gast?

1 Can I help you?
2 I'd like to order now, please.
3 What would you like to start with?
4 Would you like anything to drink?
5 Can you bring me the wine list, please?
6 What flavour would you like?
7 I'd like an ice cream, please.
8 Can I pay with a credit card?

2 Schreiben Sie passende Antworten zu den Sätzen aus Übung 1.

1 *We'd like a table for two, please.*
2 ______
3 ______
4 ______
5 ______
6 ______
7 ______
8 ______

3 Schreiben Sie passende Fragen zu den folgenden Antworten.

1 ______
Yes, I'd like cheesecake, please.

2 ______
I'm sorry, we're out of chips.

3 ______
Chocolate, please.

4 ______
I'd like pizza, please.

5 ______
Certainly, madam.

6 ______
Yes, I do. It's very good.

SOUNDS

Hören Sie sich diese Fragen an. Klingt der Sprecher höflich und freundlich?

1 Can you bring me some water, please?
2 Can I come with you?
3 I'd like an ice cream, please.
4 Can you take me to the station?
5 Can I have a German beer, please?
6 Can you turn the TV off, please?

Hören Sie noch einmal zu und wiederholen Sie. Versuchen Sie, höflich und freundlich zu klingen.

WRITING

1 Schreiben Sie einen kurzen Dialog in einem Restaurant. Verwenden Sie dabei die Sätze aus GRAMMAR Übung 1.

______

2 Beschreiben Sie in ein paar Sätzen Ihren letzten Besuch in einem Restaurant.

______

26 *Can I help you?*

GRAMMAR

1 **Ergänzen Sie die Wörter, um Reflexivpronomen zu bilden.**

my*self* your_____ him_____
her_____ it_____
our_____ your_____ them_____

2 **Ergänzen Sie die Sätze mit einem Reflexivpronomen.**

1 I often buy flowers for ___________.
2 They are building the house ___________.
3 He does all the cooking ___________.
4 You can do it ___________!
5 We enjoyed ___________ last night.

3 **Schreiben Sie Sätze mit einem Reflexivpronomen.**

He wanted some Belgian chocolates. (buy)
He bought himself some Belgian chocolates.

1 They went to a good party and had a good evening. (enjoy)
____

2 She wants to speak French. She has a self-study book. (teach)
____

3 He has nobody to talk to. (talk)
____

VOCABULARY

1 **Bilden Sie jeweils ein neues Wort mit je einem Wort aus der rechten und aus der linken Spalte.**

brief	glasses	*briefcase*
news	coat	
tooth	burger	
sun	paper	
hand	case	
rain	paste	
ham	bag	

2 **Wo kann man die Gegenstände in Übung 1 kaufen? Schreiben Sie ganze Sätze.**

1 *You can buy a briefcase in a department store.*
2 ___________
3 ___________
4 ___________
5 ___________
6 ___________
7 ___________

3 **Korrigieren Sie diese Ausdrücke.**

1 a box of shampoo ___________
2 a tube of biscuits ___________
3 a can of matches ___________
4 a bar of toothpaste ___________
5 a bottle of chocolate ___________
6 a packet of tomatoes ___________

4 **Listen Sie weitere Produkte auf, die in den Behältern aus Übung 3 angeboten werden.**

____

SOUNDS

1 Hören Sie sich die Wörter aus VOCABULARY Übung 1 an. Unterstreichen Sie die betonten Silben. Welche Regel trifft hier zu?

2 Hören Sie sich diese Sätze an und unterstreichen Sie die betonten Wörter.

1 It's too big.
2 I don't like it.
3 It doesn't suit me.
4 It doesn't fit me.
5 I don't like the colour.

Sprechen Sie die Sätze laut.

LISTENING AND FUNCTIONS

1 Hören Sie sich den Dialog an. Um was für eine Situation handelt es sich?

2 Sind die Sätze richtig oder falsch?

1 The customer wants to buy a raincoat.
2 He likes a dark blue coat.
3 It doesn't fit him.
4 It's too small.
5 There's isn't a blue coat in his size.
6 He doesn't like green because it doesn't suit him.
7 He doesn't buy the black coat because it is too big.

3 Korrigieren Sie die falschen Sätze aus Übung 2.

4 Was für Ausdrücke verwendet der Kunde, um zu sagen, dass ...

1 he wants to buy the black coat?

2 he doesn't want to buy it?

WRITING

Schreiben Sie zwei kurze Dialoge zwischen Verkäufer/in und Kunde/Kundin. Wählen Sie als Thema zwei der angegebenen Gegenstände.

sunglasses   an item of jewellery   a swimsuit   a watch

27 *Whose bag is this?*

VOCABULARY

1 Aus was für einem Stoff werden die folgenden Gegenstände normalerweise hergestellt?

binoculars ____________________

a wallet ____________________

an umbrella ____________________

a book ____________________

2 Füllen Sie das Kreuzworträtsel aus.

Across
1 You can see very far with them.
3 It keeps you dry in the rain.
5 The Lost _____ Office is where you go if you lose something.
8 Tables and chairs are often made of this material.
10 It's Peter's.
11 Silver or gold, for example.

Down
1 You put things in it.
2 It takes photos.
4 Not old.
6 You keep money in it.
7 Not thin.
9 Opposite of *in*.

SOUNDS

1 Hören Sie sich einige Wörter mit gleichlautender Endung an.

calculator camera computer leather paper rectangular umbrella

Sprechen Sie die Wörter laut.

2 Hören Sie zu und unterstreichen Sie die betonten Wörter in den Fragen und in den Antworten.

1 Are they your letters? No, they're his.
2 Is this your bag? No, it's hers.
3 Is this her umbrella? No, it's mine.
4 Is this their car? No, it's ours.
5 Is this your book? No, it's yours.
6 Is this our table? No, it's theirs.

Hören Sie noch einmal zu und sprechen Sie die Antworten laut.

GRAMMAR

1 Schreiben Sie passende Fragen zu den folgenden Sätzen.

1 ____________________
It's round.

2 ____________________
It's black.

3 ____________________
It's made of leather.

4 ____________________
No, that isn't mine.

5 ____________________
They're Janet's books.

6 ____________________
There's a purse, a box of matches and an address book in it.

2 Schreiben Sie die Sätze noch einmal mit einem Possessivpronomen.

1 It's my property. *It's mine.* ____
2 It's his car. ____
3 It's their house. ____
4 They're our binoculars. ____
5 They're her suitcases. ____
6 It's your purse. ____

READING AND WRITING

1 Welche Frage wird in den Texten beantwortet?

1 Where do you keep valuable objects?
2 How do you remember where things are?
3 What do you lose?

2 Unterstreichen Sie die Dinge, die am häufigsten verloren gehen. Wer ist am ordentlichsten?

3 Sind Sie einem der Erzähler in den Texten ähnlich? Was verlieren Sie regelmäßig?

4 Beantworten Sie die Frage in ähnlicher Weise für sich selbst.

____
____
____
____
____
____
____
____
____
____

A I lose things every day, but never very important things. I always find them again. The trouble is, when I find them it's too late. I don't need them anymore! It really is annoying. For example, I need to post a letter so I look for the stamps I bought yesterday. Of course, I can't find them so I buy some more. Every morning I spend at least ten minutes looking for my purse. I get really angry because it's always in a stupid place.

B I am usually very careful with my things. However, there are some things which I just can't keep. Umbrellas, for example. I buy two or three umbrellas every year. I put them down in shops, restaurants or in the cinema and I forget them. When I go back to get them, they're never there. Now I always buy very cheap

C I lose papers and keys – usually important papers. I also regularly leave my phone card in the telephone, and my cash card in the cashpoint machine. Last month I left my bag at the supermarket. Luckily, they phoned me and I went back to get it. Another thing I often lose is my car keys. Last week I lost them so I took the bus to work. When I got home I found them in the rubbish bin!

D I'm usually very good. I don't often lose anything. Once I left my overcoat in a restaurant but I went back the next day and they gave it to me. I never lose papers because I put them in my filing cabinet immediately. I always leave my car keys in the car so I can't lose them. I never lock the door of the house so I don't need a key and therefore I can't lose it!

28 What's the matter?

VOCABULARY

1 Schreiben Sie mindestens zwölf Körperteile auf.

____

____

____

2 Welches Bild passt zu welcher Krankheit?

a He's got a high temperature.
b She's got a cold.
c He's got a headache.
d She's got a sore finger.
e He's got toothache.

3 Was ist los? Schreiben Sie fünf mögliche Antworten auf. Verwenden Sie dabei die folgenden Verben.

hurt feel have got

1 throat ______________________
2 back ______________________
3 faint ______________________
4 dizzy ______________________
5 cough ______________________

GRAMMAR AND FUNCTIONS

1 Geben Sie den Menschen in VOCABULARY Übung 2 einen Rat.

1 *You should* ______________________
2 ______________________
3 ______________________
4 ______________________
5 ______________________

2 Schreiben Sie auf, was diese Menschen nicht tun sollten.

1 *He shouldn't* ______________________
2 ______________________
3 ______________________
4 ______________________
5 ______________________

3 Ergänzen Sie den Dialog mit den unten stehenden Sätzen.

MAN (1) ______________________
WOMAN No, I don't feel very well.
MAN (2) ______________________
WOMAN I feel sick.
MAN (3) ______________________
WOMAN And I've got a headache.
MAN (4) ______________________
WOMAN I think so. I feel very hot.

a What's the matter?
b Have you got a temperature?
c Oh dear!
d Are you all right?

Hören Sie zu und kontrollieren Sie.

4 Geben Sie der Person aus Übung 3 einen Rat.

____

____

____

SOUNDS

1 Hören Sie zu und wiederholen Sie diese Fragen.

1 Are you all right?
2 What's the matter?
3 Have you got a temperature?
4 Do you feel ill?
5 Does your back hurt?
6 What did the doctor say?

2 Wie viele Silben haben diese Wörter? Hören Sie zu und tragen Sie sie in die richtige Liste ein. Unterstreichen Sie die betonten Silben.

accident aspirin complaint exercise hospital medicine private treatment temperature

Two syllables ______________________

____

Three syllables ______________________

____

Sprechen Sie die Wörter laut.

READING AND WRITING

1 Schauen Sie sich den Text über Gesundheit im Urlaub an. Um was handelt es sich jeweils in den zwei Abschnitten?

insects water safety sun health insurance stomach problems

2 Lesen Sie den Text durch und suchen Sie die folgenden Wörter. Kontrollieren Sie, ob Sie die genaue Bedeutung wissen.

sunstroke shade symptoms mosquitoes malaria

3 Lesen Sie den Text durch. Unterstreichen Sie Ratschläge mit *should* oder *shouldn't*.

4 Schreiben Sie vier Ratschläge mit *should* oder *shouldn't*.

____

____

____

____

5 Schreiben Sie Ratschläge zu den anderen Themen in Übung 1.

Holiday health

A Many people travel to foreign countries to find the sun. So sunburn and sunstroke are common holiday complaints. You shouldn't stay in the sun too long. In very hot countries, you should stay out of the sun at midday for at least two hours. It is a good idea to sit in the shade if you can and wear a hat. If you lie in the sun you should use suncream. And remember, you can burn under water! If you stay in the sun too long without a hat, you can get sunstroke which can be quite serious. You have a high temperature and a headache. If you get these symptoms, you should lie down in a cool place, drink a lot of water and take an aspirin. If your temperature stays high, you should call a doctor.

B In some countries, insects, especially mosquitoes, are a health danger. You can wear long trousers and shirt sleeves to protect your arms and legs. You can also buy special cream to keep mosquitoes away from your body. At night, it's not a good idea to leave windows open when there are lights. In some countries, mosquitoes are dangerous because they carry malaria. When you go to these countries you should take medicine every day.

29 *Country factfile*

VOCABULARY AND SOUNDS

1 Suchen Sie 22 Adjektive in diesem Rätsel. Die Wörter können in zwei Richtungen gelesen werden (→) und (↓). Manche Buchstaben werden mehr als einmal verwendet.

H	L	O	N	G	O	O	D	Y
E	O	L	I	G	H	T	S	O
A	W	D	R	Y	B	I	G	U
V	E	I	S	H	I	G	H	N
Y	T	R	A	S	L	O	W	G
H	O	T	F	A	S	T	D	C
B	S	Y	E	A	S	Y	A	O
A	D	S	M	A	L	L	R	L
D	M	O	D	E	R	N	K	D

2 Ergänzen Sie die Aufstellung mit der Komparativ-Form und der Superlativ-Form dieser Adjektive.

	Comparative	Superlative
good	______	______
bad	______	______
heavy	______	______
old	______	______
low	______	______
easy	______	______
big	______	______
wet	______	______

3 Schreiben Sie diese Abkürzungen aus.

1 °C *degrees Centigrade*
2 m ______
3 mm ______
4 kph ______
5 km ______
6 sq km ______
7 kg ______
8 l ______

4 Ergänzen Sie die Sätze mit den richtigen Abkürzungen.

1 The average temperature in Thailand in January is 25_____.
2 The highest point in Great Britain is 1,343_____.
3 The average annual rainfall in the UK is 600_____.
4 The UK covers a land area of 242,429_____.
5 The maximum speed on motorways in France is 130_____.
6 New York City's coastline is 920_____ long.
7 One litre of water weighs 1_____.

Hören Sie zu und kontrollieren Sie.

5 Hören Sie zu und wiederholen Sie diese Maßangaben.

16°C 25 sq km 150 kph 2 kg 18°C 5,749 m
250 km 760 mm 36,790 sq km 57 kg

READING AND GRAMMAR

1 Lesen Sie den Text über Brasilien. Tragen Sie die Überschriften richtig ein.

1 Population
2 Land area
3 Climate
4 Cities
5 Rivers

2 Unterstreichen Sie die Ausdrücke, die in der Komparativ- bzw. Superlativ-Form erscheinen.

3 Korrigieren Sie diese Aussagen.

1 Brazil is bigger than Canada.
______
2 Brazil has a smaller population than Chile.
______
3 The Nile is wider than the Amazon.
______
4 Rio is bigger than São Paulo.
______
5 Most Brazilians live in the country areas.
______

4 Vergleichen Sie ...

1 Brazil and Argentina

____

2 The Amazon and the Nile

____

3 Brazil and Peru

____

4 Rio and São Paulo

____

5 June and December

____

A Brazil is the world's fourth largest country after Canada, China and the USA. It borders every country in South America except Chile and Ecuador. Its surface area is 8½ million sq km. It covers almost half of the South American continent.

B The world's second longest river is the Amazon. It is 6,300 km long. It crosses Brazil and carries 20% of the world's fresh water. It is the world's widest river and it covers the largest area.

C Brazil's population is around 140 million. It is the country with the highest population in South America and the 6th highest in the world. It is not very densely populated, with an average of only 15 people per sq km. Most of the population is concentrated along the coast and in the cities.

D Three out of four Brazilians now live in cities. São Paulo is South America's biggest city. It has over 15 million people. Rio de Janeiro, with over 10 million people is smaller than São Paulo but it is more densely populated.

E The Brazilian winter is from June to August, but it is only cold south of Rio, where the average temperature during the winter months is between 13°C and 18°C. The warmest months are from December to February. The Amazon basin receives the most rainfall, but it is not very hot – the average temperature is 27°C; but it is humid.

5 Schreiben Sie die Sätze noch einmal neu. Verwenden Sie dabei *as ... as*.

Canada is larger than the USA.
The USA is not as large as Canada.

1 São Paulo is bigger than Rio.

____

2 Rio is warmer than São Paulo.

____

3 The climate on the coast is drier than the climate in the Amazon basin.

____

4 The Nile is longer than the Amazon.

____

5 It is warmer in December than it is in June.

____

6 Schreiben Sie fünf Sätze, in denen Sie Ihr Land mit anderen Ländern vergleichen.

1 clean _______________

2 wet _______________

3 safe _______________

4 hot _______________

5 small _______________

WRITING

Schreiben Sie einen kurzen Text über Ihr Land.

____

30 Olympic spirit

VOCABULARY

1 Bilden Sie mit je einem Wort aus der rechten und linken Spalte fünf Sportarten.

hang	surfing
motor	riding
wind	ball
horse	racing
basket	gliding

2 Schreiben Sie die Wörter auf, die Sie mit den Sportarten in Übung 1 in Verbindung bringen. Sie dürfen dabei Ihr *Student's Book* verwenden.

1 ______
2 ______
3 ______
4 ______
5 ______

3 Wählen Sie ein Adjektiv, um die Sportarten in Übung 1 aus Ihrer Sicht zu beschreiben.

dangerous exciting boring fast difficult expensive fashionable tiring interesting enjoyable popular safer

______
______
______
______
______

GRAMMAR

1 Ergänzen Sie die Sätze mit *more* oder *most*.

1 Horse riding is the ______ expensive sport.
2 Baseball is ______ popular in the US than in Britain.
3 The ______ popular sport in France is cycling.
4 Hang gliding is one of the ______ dangerous sports in the world.
5 Motor racing is ______ exciting than horse racing.
6 Tennis is ______ fashionable than football.

2 Schreiben Sie Sätze, in denen Sie die Sportarten in VOCABULARY Übung 1 vergleichen.

Basketball is more popular than hang gliding.

1 ______
2 ______
3 ______
4 ______
5 ______

3 Schreiben Sie Sätze in der Superlativ-Form über die Sportarten in VOCABULARY Übung 1.

Basketball is one of the most popular sports in the world.

1 ______
2 ______
3 ______
4 ______
5 ______

4 Sind Sie mit den folgenden Aussagen einverstanden? Wie ist jeweils Ihre Meinung dazu?

1 Formula 1 motor racing is the most exciting sport in the world.

____

2 Golf is the most difficult game to understand.

____

3 Baseball is the most interesting sport I know.

____

4 The most dangerous sport is horse riding.

____

5 Skiing is not as fashionable as tennis.

____

READING AND WRITING

1 Lesen Sie den Text durch. Welcher Satz fasst am besten das Hauptthema zusammen?

1 It's important to travel to foreign countries.
2 Foreign places often seem more interesting than home.
3 Home is the best place to be.

2 Unterstreichen Sie alle Komparativ-Formen von langen Adjektiven.

3 Schreiben Sie ähnliche Sätze für die Stichwörter am Textende. Sie können dabei die folgenden Adjektive verwenden.

light tasty strange long exciting efficient friendly colourful polite

Breakfasts are lighter.

____

- The weather is better.
- The food is better – in particular, the fish is fishier, and the soups soupier.
- The light is brighter.
- The snow is whiter.
- The people are more polite and seem happier.
- The wine is cheaper.
- The buildings are more beautiful.
- The sea is warmer.
- The bars keep more civilised hours.
- The men are more good-looking and the women more sophisticated.
- The street life is livelier.
- Cakes and gateaux are more mouthwatering.
- The smells are more exotic.
- The sounds are more exciting.
- The markets are more interesting and their cheeses cheesier.
- The language is more expressive.
- The monuments are more monumental.
- The scenery is more spectacular, with the hills and mountains higher and the flat bits flatter.
- And so many ordinary things are different – breakfast, street signs, shops, clothes, children, the ringing of telephones, matches, bread, shop assistants, bank clerks – that nothing is ordinary at all.

4 Beschreiben Sie in ein paar Sätzen Ihre ersten Eindrücke von einem anderen Land. Welche Gedanken aus dem Text entsprechen auch Ihrer Meinung.

____

31 *When in Rome, do as the Romans do*

GRAMMAR

1 Wie alt muss man sein, um in Ihrem Land Folgendes machen zu dürfen?

get married
You must be sixteen years old.

1 drive a car
____

2 drive a motorbike
____

3 go into a bar without an adult
____

4 vote
____

5 buy cigarettes
____

6 leave school
____

2 Welche Vorschrift passt zu welcher Situation?

1 You mustn't smoke or use a computer during take off and landing. ☐
2 You mustn't give food to the animals. ☐
3 You mustn't leave your bags unattended. ☐
4 You must have a shower before you go in. ☐
5 You must keep dogs on a lead. ☐
6 You must wear a seat belt. ☐
7 You mustn't talk. ☐
8 You mustn't use your hands. ☐

a in an exam
b in a park
c in a car
d at a zoo
e during a football match
f at an airport
g at a swimming pool
h in a plane

3 Ergänzen Sie die Sätze mit *must* oder *mustn't*.

1 You __________ make a noise in a library.
2 You __________ walk on the grass.
3 You __________ have a visa to enter some countries.
4 You __________ go into a pub without an adult.
5 You __________ smoke in the classroom.
6 You __________ take your shoes off when you go into a mosque.
7 You __________ always carry your identity card in some countries.
8 You __________ take a mobile phone into exams.

4 Handelt es sich bei den Sätzen in Übung 3 um Vorschriften oder um gute Ratschläge?

5 Schreiben Sie je eine weitere Vorschrift für die Situationen in Übung 2.

1 _______________
2 _______________
3 _______________
4 _______________
5 _______________
6 _______________
7 _______________
8 _______________

READING

1 Schauen Sie sich die Informationstafeln an. Wo würde man sie jeweils vorfinden?

1 Town park
2 Golf club
3 Public library
4 Swimming pool

2 Lesen Sie die Informationstafel A. Schreiben Sie jeweils die entsprechende Vorschrift unter das passende Bild.

A *You are not allowed to climb the trees.*

B ____________________

C ____________________

D ____________________

E ____________________

F ____________________

A

Opening hours:
8 am to 8 pm from 1st October to 30th April
10 am to 10 pm from 1st May to 30th September
RULES:
put litter in bins
no golf
no cycling
keep your dog on a lead
You are not allowed to:
– sleep overnight on the benches
– stay inside after closing time
– walk on the flower beds
– climb the trees

3 Lesen Sie die Informationstafel B. Unterstreichen Sie zwei Sätze mit *must* oder *mustn't*.

4 Schreiben Sie weitere Vorschriften mit *must* oder *mustn't* für beide Informationstafeln.

Notice A
You mustn't play golf in the park.

Notice B
You mustn't wear shorts.

WRITING

Schreiben Sie Vorschriften für die anderen beiden Orte in READING Übung 1.

____
____
____
____
____
____
____
____
____
____

B

Opening hours:
10 am to 7.30 pm on weekdays
9 am to 9.30 pm at weekends
Rules:
– you must wear proper swimsuits
– shorts are not allowed
– an adult must stay with children under six at all times
– no running or jumping
– no smoking in the pool area
– food and drink are not allowed near the pool

32 Have you ever been to London?

READING

1 Lesen Sie den Text. Listen Sie die Jobs auf, die Jane ausgeübt hat.

a model ____________________

____

2 Unterstreichen Sie die Sätze im Perfekt.

3 Suchen Sie drei Sätze in der einfachen Vergangenheit.

Jobs are my career

Jane Brooks has had fifty-four jobs in four years and still hasn't found her ideal career. She has been a model, a waitress, an actress, a nanny and a ticket seller. The shortest job she had was as a cook in a canteen. She left it after just two hours. The longest job she had was as a zoo-keeper. She stayed in that job for two months.

Jane, 23, of Southampton, is now working in telesales. She says, 'I just haven't found a career I really enjoy. I'll keep trying different jobs until I do.'

GRAMMAR

1 Ordnen Sie die Wörter in zwei Gruppen ein. Manche Wörter gehören in beide Gruppen.

ate been drunk had driven read left saw flown wore taken bought made went written sold fought met found took eaten flew drove gone wrote seen worn

Past participle ____________________

____

Past simple ____________________

____

2 Bringen Sie die Wörter in die richtige Reihenfolge, um Sätze zu bilden.

1 a you been ever country to have foreign?

____

2 has he on never television appeared.

____

3 visited I a lot have countries of.

____

4 Spain went last they year to.

____

5 did Spain when go they to?

____

3 Ergänzen Sie die Fragen mit einem passenden Partizip Perfekt aus der Liste in Übung 1. Beantworten Sie die Fragen mit einer *yes*- oder *no*-Antwort.

Have you ever *been* to a football match?
Yes, I have.

1 Have you ever __________ champagne?

____

2 Have you ever __________ a Mercedes?

____

3 Have you ever __________ a film star?

____

4 Have you ever __________ a hat?

____

5 Have you ever __________ in a plane?

____

6 Have you ever __________ traditional English food?

____

7 Have you ever __________ a book?

____

8 Have you ever __________ an exam?

____

4 Wählen Sie die richtige Verbform.

1 I *have never been/never went* to Japan.
2 We *went/have gone* to stay with my aunt last year.
3 He *has found/find* an interesting job at last.
4 I *have met/met* her last week.
5 She *has never flown/never flew* in a plane before.
6 She *has drunk/drank* champagne on her birthday.

5 Ergänzen Sie die Dialoge mit *gone*, *been* oder *went*.

1 A Have you ever __________ to Russia?
  B Yes, I have. I __________ there last summer.
2 A Where's Peter __________? I've phoned him three times this week and he's not at home.
  B He's __________ to Brussels on business. I think he __________ on Monday. He'll be back at the weekend.

LISTENING

1 Schreiben Sie die Dinge oder Städte auf, die Sie mit diesen Ländern in Verbindung bringen.

Russia ______________________________
Australia ______________________________
Switzerland ______________________________
Mexico ______________________________
Japan ______________________________

2 Hören Sie sich das folgende Gespräch an. Welche Länder wurden jeweils besucht?

Man ______________________________
Woman ______________________________

3 Hören Sie noch einmal zu. Machen Sie jeweils ein Häkchen neben die Dinge, Orte oder Städte, die gesehen oder besucht wurden.

kangaroos ☐	Moscow ☐
Lake Constance ☐	surfing beaches ☐
mountain scenery ☐	Red Square ☐
Sydney Opera House ☐	Zürich ☐
the Kremlin ☐	a ski resort ☐

4 Beschreiben Sie in vier Sätzen, was gesehen bzw. besucht wurde.

WRITING

1 Schauen Sie den Text in READING noch einmal an. Schreiben Sie einen ähnlichen Text über Ihr Arbeitsleben.

2 Hören Sie sich das Gespräch in LISTENING noch einmal an. Beschreiben Sie in ein paar Zeilen Ihre Reiseerfahrungen. Erzählen Sie, wo Sie gewesen sind, was Sie dort gesehen haben und was nicht.

33 What's happened?

SOUNDS

1 Hören Sie zu und wiederholen Sie diese Fragen. Achten Sie auf die Betonung.

1 Have you seen the doctor yet?
2 Have you ever met her?
3 Have they done the shopping yet?
4 Has he been here before?
5 Has she bought her ticket?

2 Hören Sie zu und wiederholen Sie diese Wörter.

break crashed drilled dropped crossed parked scored

3 Wie wird das a in diesen Wörtern ausgesprochen? Ordnen Sie die Wörter in drei Gruppen ein.

age back park bag car crash exam face pay plate sharp stay take

/eɪ/ *age* ____________________
/æ/ *back* ____________________
/ɑː/ *park* ____________________

Hören Sie zu und kontrollieren Sie. Sprechen Sie die Wörter laut.

GRAMMAR AND VOCABULARY

1 Schreiben Sie jeweils das Partizip Perfekt dieser unregelmäßigen Verben auf.

steal ____________
fall ____________
leave ____________
come ____________
keep ____________
break ____________
run ____________
catch ____________
hurt ____________
pay ____________
lose ____________
find ____________

2 Ergänzen Sie die Sätze mit einem Verb im Perfekt. Wählen Sie aus der Liste in Übung 1.

1 He's at the police station because someone ____________ his car.
2 She isn't playing tennis because she ____________ a bad cold.
3 They ____________ their cat and they're looking everywhere for it.
4 Why's he crying? Because he ____________ off his bicycle.
5 Look, I ____________ someone's wallet on the ground.
6 I'm afraid, I ____________ the glass. I dropped it.

3 Ergänzen Sie die Sätze mit der richtigen Zeitform. Machen Sie ein Häkchen, wenn Sie das Perfekt verwenden und ein Kreuzchen, wenn Sie die einfache Vergangenheit verwenden.

a to talk about experiences ☐
I ____________ (never, visit) South America.

b to talk about a definite time in the past ☐
I ____________ (visit) Spain last summer.

c to talk about an action which happened at an indefinite time in the past ☐
I ____________ (read) that book. It's very good.

d for a recent action with *just* ☐
I ____________ (just, had) a big meal.

e in questions with *yet* ☐
____________ (do) your homework yet?

f for a past action which has a result in the present ☐
I'm taking him to the doctor's because he ____________ (hurt) his leg.

g in questions with *when* ☐
When ____________ (go) to Spain?

h to describe a series of actions in the past ☐
First we ____________ (visit) the museum then we ____________ (have) lunch.

4 Ergänzen Sie die Sätze mit der richtigen Zeitform.

1 We (go) ____________ to France for a holiday last summer.
2 I (lose) ____________ my credit card so I'm afraid I can't pay for the meal.
3 I don't think she (ever visit) ____________ California.
4 When (come back) ____________ from your business trip?
5 (take) ____________ your exam yet?
6 We (go) ____________ to Barcelona then we (take) ____________ a train to Valencia. It was wonderful!
7 We (just, book) ____________ a table at the Lebanese restaurant. Are you coming with us?

5 Beantworten Sie die folgenden Fragen.

Have you ever met a film star?
Yes, I have. I met Sean Connery when I was ten.

1 Have you ever stolen anything?
____
2 Have you ever lost anything important?
____
3 Have you ever broken something valuable?
____
4 Have you ever taken part in a sports competition?
____
5 Have you ever hurt yourself badly?
____
6 Have you ever found something in the street?
____

READING AND LISTENING

1 Ergänzen Sie das Gespräch mit den unten stehenden Sätzen (a bis d).

JAN Hi, Pete!
PETE Oh, hello, Jan. (1) ____________
JAN Great! I've been at the office all day and I've met the new director. What about you? You look very tired.(2) ____________
PETE Awful! I've only just finished the housework.
JAN Oh dear. I am sorry.
PETE I'm afraid (3) ____________
JAN That doesn't matter. I can take it tomorrow.
PETE Are you very hungry? I haven't made dinner yet.
JAN Oh. Well. (4) ____________
PETE I'm sorry, I haven't had time.
JAN Well, how about going out to eat?
PETE That's a great idea!

a I haven't taken the car to the garage yet
b What sort of day have you had?
c Have you done any shopping?
d Have you had a good day?

2 Hören Sie zu und kontrollieren Sie.

3 Korrigieren Sie diese Sätze.

1 Pete has had a good day.
____
2 Jan has travelled all day.
____
3 Pete is tired because he has had a long day at work.
____
4 Jan has just arrived home from the supermarket.
____
5 Pete has taken the car to the garage and done the shopping.
____
6 Pete has made the evening meal.
____

34 Planning a perfect day

VOCABULARY

1 Füllen Sie das Picknick-Kreuzworträtsel aus.

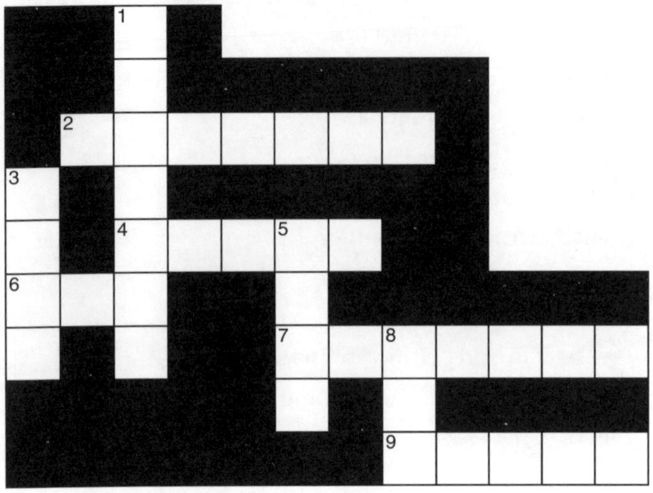

Across
2 You need them to light a barbecue.
4 You need one to cut things.
6 This keeps things cool.
7 You should take this home.
9 Bottles are made of this

Down
1 Comfortable to sit on.
3 Choose a sunny day when there is no _____.
5 You need this to eat with.
8 You put everything in one.

2 Welche Anweisung oder welcher Ratschlag passt zu welcher Situation?

Don't worry!	☐	Slow down!	☐
Be careful!	☐	Please sit down.	☐
Be quiet!	☐	Excuse me.	☐

1 Your friend is standing in the road and doesn't see a car coming.
2 Your friend is driving too fast.
3 Your guests arrive and you take them into the sitting room.
4 You need to interrupt someone.
5 Your friend has an exam.
6 You are a teacher and you walk into a noisy classroom.

GRAMMAR

1 Fügen Sie die beiden passenden Satzteile zusammen.

1	You go to the chemist's	a	to visit the town.
2	He went to Britain	b	to get a visa.
3	I bought a guide book	c	to buy aspirin.
4	She went to the post office	d	to study economics.
5	He is going to university	e	to learn English.
6	You go to the consulate	f	to get a stamp.

2 Erklären Sie, warum Sie diese Aktivitäten tun.

read the newspaper
I read the newspaper to find out what is happening in the world.

1 go to the bank
____

2 go to a travel agent
____

3 you are taking an English course
____

4 go to an art gallery
____

5 go to a bookshop
____

6 go on holiday
____

3 Warum werden diese Länder/Städte besucht? Sie können die folgenden Wörter verwenden.

scenery mountains surf kangaroos islands ski gondola relax sun wildlife

Canada *People visit Canada to see spectacular scenery.*
Venice _______________
Switzerland _______________
Greece _______________
Australia _______________

LISTENING

1 Hören Sie sich die folgenden vier kurzen Gespräche an. Wo fahren oder gehen die Menschen hin? Tragen Sie die entsprechende Gesprächsnummer ein.

the airport	☐	the station	☐
the restaurant	☐	the pub	☐
Kenya	☐	the supermarket	☐

2 Hören Sie noch einmal zu. Warum fahren oder gehen die Menschen dorthin? Verwenden Sie *to* + die Grundform des Verbs.

1 ____________________
____

2 ____________________
____

3 ____________________
____

4 ____________________
____

READING AND WRITING

1 Schauen Sie sich die Textüberschrift an. Fliegt der Autor gerne?

2 Achten Sie darauf, dass Sie die unterstrichenen Wörter im Text alle verstehen. Sie dürfen Ihr Wörterbuch verwenden.

3 Lesen Sie die Überschriften A bis E durch. Welche Überschrift passt zu welchem Absatz im Text?

A Eat if you must ☐
B Travel as light as you can ☐
C Avoid agitation ☐
D Have something to do ☐
E Don't queue unnecessarily ☐

4 Geben Sie ein paar Ratschläge für die folgenden Situationen.

going on a camping holiday
buying a new computer   taking an exam

Advice to make travelling by plane less unpleasant

1
The most sensible travellers find somewhere comfortable to spend their time in the airport and they get on the plane last.

2
You can walk miles in an airport so don't carry too much hand luggage. Leave your camera in your suitcase and don't buy duty-free goods.

3
If you like crosswords, you will never get a better opportunity. Knit. Play Travel Scrabble. Write letters. Do things you don't usually have time to do.

4
This is good for passing time but remember, the food is usually disgusting at airports.

5
Don't get upset if the plane is late because that's normal: sit back and keep calm. Read a book or talk to other people.

35 She sings well

VOCABULARY AND GRAMMAR

1 **Schreiben Sie das Gegenteil zu diesen Adjektiven auf.**

good *bad*
quiet ____________
careful ____________
polite ____________
fast ____________
early ____________

2 **Schreiben Sie das Adverb (Umstandswort) zu diesen Adjektiven auf.**

good ____________
bad ____________
happy ____________
fast ____________
easy ____________
early ____________
angry ____________
late ____________
careless ____________
fluent ____________
clear ____________
patient ____________

3 **Ergänzen Sie die Sätze mit einem Adjektiv oder einem Adverb aus Übung 2. Es gibt möglicherweise mehr als eine Antwort.**

1 I speak French quite ____________ but I make a lot of grammatical mistakes.
2 My spelling is quite ____________ but my intonation is very ____________.
3 When I don't understand something my teacher explains it ____________.
4 He's a ____________ person. He is always smiling.
5 She's very ____________ to understand because she speaks very ____________.
6 I sometimes arrive ____________ for work.

4 **Schreiben Sie Adverbien auf, die zu diesen Verben passen.**

1 shout *loudly*
2 sing ____________
3 drive ____________
4 cook ____________
5 swim ____________
6 speak English ____________
7 laugh ____________

5 **Schreiben Sie je einen Satz mit jedem Verb aus Übung 4. Verwenden Sie dabei eines Ihrer notierten Adverbien.**

1 ____________
2 ____________
3 ____________
4 ____________
5 ____________
6 ____________
7 ____________

6 **Ergänzen Sie das Schulzeugnis mit passenden Adjektiven oder Adverbien.**

Maria's English is quite ____________. She works ____________ and behaves very ____________ in class. Her writing is ____________ but her spelling is very ____________. She speaks quite ____________ but her intonation is not very ____________. If she continues to work ____________, she should pass the exam ________.

LISTENING

1 Hören Sie sich das folgende Gespräch an. Machen Sie ein Häkchen neben die Tätigkeiten, die angesprochen werden.

skiing	☐	dancing	☐
driving	☐	swimming	☐
cooking	☐	speaking English	☐
singing	☐	speaking in public	☐

2 Hören Sie noch einmal zu und ergänzen Sie die Sätze.

1 She can swim quite ________ but she can't swim very ________.
2 She's quite a ________ dancer.
3 She cooks very ________.
4 She drives too ________ in town and too ________ on the motorway.
5 She's a ________ driver.

3 Schauen Sie sich die Liste in Übung 1 an. Wie gut machen Sie diese Sachen? Schreiben Sie zu jedem Thema einen Satz.

____
____
____
____
____
____

READING

1 Lesen Sie den Text über Italien durch. Der Autor vergleicht Norditalien mit Süditalien. Welche Gegend gefällt ihm besser?

2 Unterstreichen Sie alle Adverbien im Text. Prüfen Sie, ob Sie deren Bedeutung jeweils richtig verstehen. Sie dürfen Ihr Wörterbuch verwenden.

3 Listen Sie vier Dinge auf, die für die Norditaliener typisch sind.

They wear expensive designer clothes.
____
____
____

4 Listen Sie vier Dinge auf, die für die Süditaliener typisch sind.

They sit for hours in cafes.
____
____
____
____

After southern Italy, Milan didn't seem Italian at all. People walked quickly and purposefully, wearing expensive designer clothes. They didn't sit for hours in cafés drinking espressos and eating mountains of pasta. They didn't argue passionately about unimportant things. They took life seriously. They had meetings. They did business. They talked on car phones. They drove slowly, mostly in BMWs and Porsches and they parked carefully. The women all looked like *Vogue* models. It was like a town of southern California in Italy. But this was Italy. And I wanted the noisy street life, washing hanging across the streets, people shouting noisily, scooters honking their horns ...

WRITING

Schauen Sie sich den Text im Abschnitt READING an. Schreiben Sie einen ähnlichen Text über die Einwohner einer Stadt, die Sie kennen.

____
____
____
____
____

36 *I'll go by train*

VOCABULARY AND READING

1 Bilden Sie neue Wörter oder Ausdrücke, indem Sie Wörter aus Kästchen A mit Wörtern aus Kästchen B verbinden.

A	B
passport first check departure petrol baggage ticket arrival boarding	reclaim office station class hall lounge control pass in

____

____

____

____

____

2 Diese Sätze beschreiben den Ablauf einer Flugreise. Bringen Sie sie in die richtige Reihenfolge.

a You show your boarding pass to the steward and you board the plane.
b You go through passport control, through customs and into the arrival hall.
c It's usual to book your flight.
d The plane lands.
e You leave your luggage at the check-in and they give you a boarding pass.
f You wait in the departure lounge until they call your flight, and then go to the right gate.
g The plane takes off.
h It's important to go to the right terminal if you want to be on time.
i You go through passport control.

3 Um welches Verkehrsmittel handelt es sich jeweils bei den folgenden Sätzen?

Train ______________________________

Plane ______________________________

Car ______________________________

Boat ______________________________

1 I love travelling but I hate aircraft, airports, air terminals and everything to do with them.
2 It's often expensive to have a full meal on a train and the food is often bad.
3 I'd like to travel everywhere by rail because it's so relaxing.
4 It is more and more difficult to get a drink on a short flight.
5 To drive in many countries you need to get an international licence.
6 I love arriving in a city by river. For example, it's wonderful to go down the Danube to Budapest.
7 You should buy a good road map before you start your journey.
8 It is still possible to travel by rail in comfort.
9 It's a good idea to stop for a rest every two hours when you are on a long journey.
10 When the sea is rough it can be very uncomfortable.

4 Machen Sie ein Häkchen neben die Sätze in Übung 3, die Positives über das Verkehrsmittel zum Ausdruck bringen und ein Kreuzchen neben die Sätze, die etwas Negatives bedeuten.

5 Schreiben Sie positive und negative Anmerkungen zum Fahrrad als Verkehrsmittel.

____

____

____

____

____

____

SOUNDS

Hören Sie zu und machen Sie jeweils ein Häkchen neben die Sätze, die Sie hören.

1 a I won't take the train.
  b I want to take the train.
2 a I'll buy a return ticket.
  b I buy a return ticket.
3 a We'll stay here tonight.
  b Will you stay here tonight?
4 a You'll like this restaurant.
  b You like this restaurant.
5 a I'll check my flight.
  b I check my flight.

Hören Sie noch einmal zu und kontrollieren Sie.

GRAMMAR AND LISTENING

1 Bringen Sie die Wörter in die richtige Reihenfolge, um Fragen zu bilden.

1 he go will sightseeing when?

____

2 you single have a will room?

____

3 will long in how you stay London?

____

4 the you will get from hotel the airport to how?

____

5 evening will have where you dinner this?

____

2 Welche Antwort passt jeweils zu den Fragen in Übung 1?

a For a week. d At the weekend.
b By taxi. e No, a double.
c At home.

3 Schreiben Sie fünf Dinge auf, die Sie diese Woche erledigen werden, sofern Sie Zeit dazu haben.

I'll wash the car.

1 ______________________
2 ______________________
3 ______________________
4 ______________________
5 ______________________

4 Hören Sie das folgende Gespräch an. Um welche Situation handelt es sich?

a Choosing an evening's television
b Sightseeing
c Planning an evening out

5 Hören Sie noch einmal zu. Korrigieren Sie diese Sätze.

1 She'll stay in bed until 10 o'clock.

____

2 She won't have breakfast.

____

3 She'll visit the Louvre in the afternoon.

____

4 She'll have lunch at the hotel.

____

5 She'll go up the Eiffel Tower in the morning.

____

6 Schreiben Sie vier weitere Dinge auf, die sie noch machen wird. Verwenden Sie dabei diese Wörter.

Notre Dame Cathedral Montmartre district
shopping for souvenirs glass of wine

1 ______________________
2 ______________________
3 ______________________
4 ______________________

WRITING

Stellen Sie sich vor, Sie zeigen einem Gast Ihre Stadt oder Ihr Land. Schreiben Sie in ein paar Sätzen, wo Sie hingehen und was Sie unternehmen werden.

____
____
____
____
____
____
____

37 *What will it be like in the future?*

VOCABULARY

1 Schreiben Sie die Adjektive zu diesen Substantiven (Hauptwörtern) auf. Sie dürfen dabei Ihr Wörterbuch verwenden.

sun ________	cloud ________
rain ________	fog ________
cold ________	heat ________
wind ________	warmth ________
snow ________	wet ________

2 Welche Bedeutung (1 - 6) haben die Symbole A - F?

A

B

C

D

E

F

1 Sunshine	4 Thunderstorm
2 Temperature	5 Rain
3 Snow	6 Wind speed and direction

3 Was ist das ideale Wetter für die folgenden Tätigkeiten ?

having a picnic ________

sailing ________

a seaside holiday ________

growing tomatoes ________

working indoors ________

SOUNDS

Hören Sie zu. Unterstreichen Sie die Temperaturen, die Sie hören.

11°C -8°C 27°C 0°C -1°C 16°C 19°C -3°C
35°C 7°C -4°C 13°C 24°C -10°C

Sprechen Sie die Temperaturen laut.

GRAMMAR

1 Schauen Sie sich die Wetterkarte für morgen an. Wie wird das Wetter in den folgenden Gegenden?

1 Venice ________

2 Naples ________

3 Milan ________

4 Sicily ________

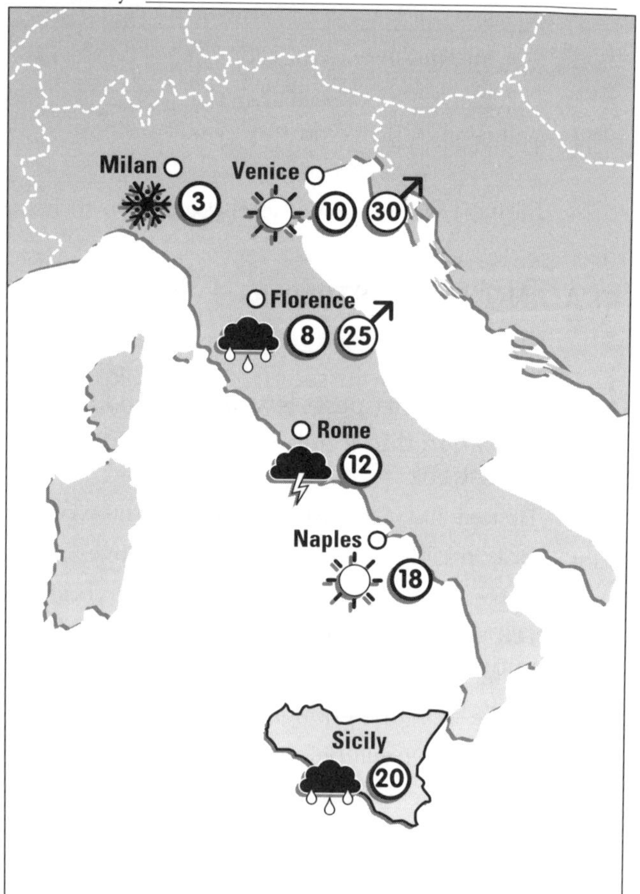

2 Beschreiben Sie das Wetter in den Gegenden in Übung 1. Verwenden Sie dabei *won't*.

It won't be sunny and warm. It won't be a nice day.

1 ______
2 ______
3 ______
4 ______

3 Wie ist heute das Wetter bei Ihnen? Wie wird es in den nächsten paar Tagen sein? Schreiben Sie dazu ein paar Sätze.

4 Ergänzen Sie die Sätze mit einem Verb in der Zukunftsform.

1 In the future the world ______ warmer.
2 Many cities ______ underwater.
3 In Britain snow at Christmas ______ very rare.
4 Crops ______ more quickly in the hotter climate.
5 Temperatures ______ by 2–6°C.
6 Ice at the North Pole ______.

READING AND LISTENING

1 Lesen Sie die Voraussagen für die Zukunft. Schreiben Sie O neben die optimistischen Voraussagen und P neben die pessimistischen Voraussagen.

1 There will be too many people in the world.
2 Most people will live more healthy lives.
3 There won't be enough food for everyone.
4 The world economy will get better.
5 Farmers will produce more crops.
6 There won't be enough petrol.
7 Fresh water will be very expensive.
8 Many big cities will disappear underwater.
9 People will live longer and happier lives.
10 There will be fewer species of wild animals.

2 Hören Sie sich das folgende Gespräch an. Wer blickt der Zukunft optimistisch entgegen? Wer ist eher pessimistisch?

3 Hören Sie noch einmal zu. Machen Sie ein Häkchen neben die Voraussagen, die auch in Übung 1 erscheinen.

4 Sehen Sie der Zukunft eher optimistisch oder eher pessimistisch entgegen? Mit welchen Voraussagen stimmen Sie überein?

WRITING

1 Schreiben Sie ein paar Voraussagen über die Zukunft unserer Welt.

2 Schreiben Sie ein paar Voraussagen über Ihr eigenes Leben für das kommende Jahr.

I'll be able to speak English quite well.

38 *Hamlet was written by Shakespeare*

SOUNDS

1 Schauen Sie sich das Beispiel an. Korrigieren Sie die Sätze.

1 Tea is grown in Brazil. (India)
No, it isn't. It's grown in India.

2 The telephone was invented by Marconi. (Bell)
______

3 *Guernica* was painted by Monet. (Picasso)
______

4 *Hamlet* was written by Spencer. (Shakespeare)
______

5 Toyota cars are made in the United States. (Japan)
______

6 The Pyramids were built by Alexander the Great. (The Pharaohs)
______

Hören Sie zu und korrigieren Sie Ihre Antworten.

2 Unterstreichen Sie die betonten Silben in diesen Wörtern.

pottery computer tobacco coffee compose invent discover Japanese consume appreciate introduce

Hören Sie zu und kontrollieren Sie Ihre Antworten.

VOCABULARY AND GRAMMAR

1 Ordnen Sie die Wörter aus der Liste den Verben zu, mit denen Sie sie verwenden würden.

rice house Halley's comet oranges Australia potatoes dynamite mosque telephone church Jupiter coffee penicillin the Pyramids cotton

invent ______
grow ______
discover ______
build ______

2 Ergänzen Sie die Sätze mit Verben aus Übung 1.

1 They ______ rice in Vietnam.
2 Sultan Ahmed ______ the Blue Mosque in Istanbul.
3 Fleming ______ penicillin in 1928.
4 The Spanish ______ oranges in the region of Valencia.
5 The Europeans ______ Australia in the 17th century.
6 The Chinese ______ gunpowder in the 9th century.

3 Machen Sie ein Häkchen neben die Sätze in Übung 2, die im Präsens (in der Gegenwart) geschrieben sind und ein Kreuzchen neben die Sätze, die im Präteritum (in der Vergangenheit) geschrieben sind.

4 Schreiben Sie die Sätze in Übung 2 noch einmal neu in der Passiv-Form.

1 *Rice is grown in Vietnam.*
2 ______
3 ______
4 ______
5 ______
6 ______

5 Schreiben Sie fünf weitere Sätze in der Passiv-Form. Verwenden Sie dabei die Verben aus Übung 1.

1 ______
2 ______
3 ______
4 ______
5 ______

6 Schreiben Sie die Namen auf von jeweils zwei ...

famous paintings ______
songs or pieces of music ______
famous buildings ______
books you like ______

7 Schreiben Sie Sätze in der Passiv-Form über die in Übung 6 genannten Dinge.

The Mona Lisa was painted by Leonardo da Vinci.

READING AND WRITING

1 Schreiben Sie das Partizip Perfekt zu diesen Verben auf. Kontrollieren Sie, ob Sie die Bedeutung jeweils kennen.

drink ______
introduce ______
appreciate ______
grow ______
sell ______
dry ______
enjoy ______
consume ______
heat ______

2 Lesen Sie Text A über Tee und unterstreichen Sie alle Verben in der Passiv-Form. Sie dürfen dabei ein Wörterbuch verwenden.

3 Lesen Sie die Texte B und C. Wissen Sie, worum es sich jeweils bei *it* handelt?

4 Was halten Ihre Landsleute von diesen Produkten? Wann und wie werden sie konsumiert? Schreiben Sie zu jedem Produkt ein paar Zeilen.

A

Tea comes from a tree which is grown in countries where the climate is warm and quite wet. The leaves are dried and heated. It was first grown as a commercial crop in China in the 8th century. It was introduced into Europe in the 17th century. Today it is grown in India, China and Sri Lanka and it is sold to countries all over the world.

B

Half a billion cups of *it* are drunk in the world every day.
It was introduced to Europe in the 17th century and was for a long time enjoyed only by rich people. Today *it* is mostly grown in South America and eastern Africa.
It is now one of the most popular hot drinks in Europe. On average, in Scandinavia, 10.5 kg are drunk per person each year. Only 3.5 kg are drunk in southern Europe.
It is drunk at the start of each day and after each meal.
It is appreciated by workers because *it* helps them concentrate.
Many people don't drink *it* in the evening because *it* keeps them awake.
Nobody really knows if *it* is good or bad for your health but almost everybody drinks *it*.

C

It was first consumed by native people in Latin America.
It was introduced into Spain and Portugal in the 16th century.
In the 17th century *it* was grown in North America and *it* was sold all over the world.
Today, a large part of the world crop is still grown in North and South America.
It is well known that *it* is bad for your health, but many people all over the world continue to smoke *it*.
In many countries *it* cannot be consumed in public places. In restaurants and bars there are areas where *it* can be consumed. And it is forbidden to sell *it* to children.

39 *She said it wasn't far*

GRAMMAR

1 Schreiben Sie, was die Menschen tatsächlich gesagt haben.

1 She said it was open all year.

____

2 He said it started at half past nine.

____

3 He said that dinner was served at seven.

____

4 They said they were late because of the traffic.

____

5 She said she didn't like the food.

____

6 She said she wasn't staying another night.

____

2 Unterstreichen Sie die richtige Zeitform des Verbs.

1 He said he *was/is* in Brighton.
2 'The last train *leaves/left* at 9.30 on Saturdays,' she said.
3 She said it *costs/cost* fifteen pounds a night.
4 They said they *were/are* taking the first flight.
5 The receptionist said that dinner *was/is* at 7 o'clock.
6 'Dinner *is/was* at 7 o'clock,' said the receptionist.
7 They said it *was/is* only three kilometres from the hotel.
8 He said he *finishes/finished* the language course this week.

3 Schreiben Sie die Sätze noch einmal neu in der indirekten Rede.

1 'It's not far from the town centre,' said John.

____

2 'I don't like opera,' she said.

____

3 'The bus arrives at 9 o'clock,' she said.

____

4 'We've got a double room,' said the manager.

____

5 'It costs thirty pounds a night,' he said.

____

6 'The train takes half an hour,' she said.

____

7 'We don't want a television in the room,' they said.

____

8 'We're early. It doesn't leave until six thirty,' he said.

____

VOCABULARY

Denken Sie über diese Situationen nach. Schreiben Sie Wörter und Ausdrücke auf, die man in diesen Situationen verwenden kann.

a informing of a flat to buy

____

____

b informing of a flight delay

____

____

c informing of arrangements to go to a concert

____

____

d changing a lunch appointment

____

____

LISTENING AND READING

1 Hören Sie sich die folgenden vier Telefongespräche an. Welches Gespräch passt zu welcher Situation im Abschnitt VOCABULARY?

Phone call 1 ________

Phone call 2 ________

Phone call 3 ________

Phone call 4 ________

2 Hören Sie noch einmal zu. Nehmen Sie die Nachricht jeweils schriftlich entgegen.

Phone call 1 *John Griffiths called; has tickets; concert at Palace Hall 8.30*

Phone call 2 ________________

Phone call 3 ________________

Phone call 4 ________________

3 Schauen Sie sich Ihre Notizen zu Übung 2 an. Unterstreichen Sie die Fehler in der folgenden Nachricht.

> *John Griffiths called. He said he had the tickets for you both. He said the concert was at the Palace Hall and it started at 8.00. He said he was taking the train because it was cheaper and it left at 7 o'clock. He said he was in the office all day if you wanted to phone him.*

4 Korrigieren Sie die Fehler in der Nachricht zu Telefongespräch 1.

____

____

____

____

____

5 Die Nachrichten zu den Telefongesprächen 2 und 3 sind durcheinander gebracht worden. Können Sie sie richtig zuordnen?

> *Maria phoned to say she had a dentist's appointment at 1.30 tomorrow. Mrs Croft phoned to say she was at Charles de Gaulle Airport in Paris and her flight was delayed. She said she could meet you for coffee at 11 in Ascari's. She said she didn't know when she would arrive in London. She said you didn't need to meet her because she would get a taxi home. She said that if you didn't phone back she would see you there tomorrow at 11. She also said she had got the books you needed for college. She said that the new office over there was fine and the new manager seemed competent. And they only cost £5 each.*

WRITING

Lesen Sie die Nachricht zu Telefongespräch 1 noch einmal. Schreiben Sie das Gespräch auf.

A Can I speak to Peter, please? This is John Griffiths.

B I'm sorry, he's out at the moment. Can I take a message?

A ________________

____

____

B ________________

40 Dear Jan… Love Ruth

READING

1 Lesen Sie den Brief. Suchen Sie die Antworten zu diesen Fragen.

1. Who is writing?
2. Who is she writing to?
3. Where is she?
4. Why is she there?

2 Fügen Sie diese Sätze jeweils an der richtigen Stelle im Brief ein.

a I'd like to find a job at the seaside.
b Last Saturday we went sightseeing to London for the day.
c Luckily, they are Czech so we speak English together.
d It was my first trip on a boat and I was ill!

3 Suchen Sie je ein Beispiel für jede Zeitform des Verbs.

Dear Anna,
I'm sorry I haven't written to you earlier but I have been very busy. As you know, I left home on 5th April and I travelled by train and ferry to Britain. The ferry journey wasn't very nice because there was a lot of wind. (1) I won't travel on one again!
The language school here in Hastings is very good and I'm enjoying the classes. We work every morning from nine to one o'clock. In the afternoon there are organised visits and group activities. (2) I saw all the places I've seen pictures of in my English books.
I'm staying with a family who are very kind to me. There are two other students from my course staying here, too. (3) In the evenings we go to a pub or a disco. I've met lots of other students of different nationalities.
The course finishes at the end of June. I don't know exactly what I'll do in the summer. I think I'll stay here in Britain for July. (4) It'll be easier then because I hope my English will be better than it is now!
Love from
Maria

GRAMMAR

1 Unterstreichen Sie die Verben in diesen Sätzen. Welche Zeitform des Verbs wird jeweils verwendet? Sie dürfen dabei Ihr Student's Book verwenden.

1. Jan went to Mario's room.
   ____
2. I'm staying with the Hawkins family.
   ____
3. I'll come to see you in the summer.
   ____
4. They haven't met many foreigners.
   ____
5. I like dancing.
   ____

2 Fügen Sie die beiden passenden Satzteile zusammen.

1. I'll come with you this afternoon
2. The man came out of the pub
3. I haven't visited Westminster
4. I like sightseeing
5. She's sitting in the bar

a because I've never been to London.
b if I finish my homework this morning.
c when the weather is good.
d waiting for you.
e and walked across the road.

3 Unterstreichen Sie die Wörter, die sowohl das einfache Präteritum (die einfache Vergangenheit) als auch das Partizip Perfekt bedeuten.

won spoke bought said stepped went sold
came sent told eaten drank got made
arrived left lost stolen been took read
saw flew written climbed gone hurt found

4 **Perfekt oder einfache Vergangenheit? Wählen Sie die richtige Zeitform.**

1 He ______________ Ruth at a disco last Saturday. (meet)

2 She ______________ from a holiday in Spain. (just, come back)

3 I ______________ my car key. Can you help me find it? (lose)

4 He ______________ an award for the film in 1968. (win)

5 ______________ you ______________ this book by Thomas Hardy? It's very good. (read)

6 They ______________ in Britain two weeks ago. (arrive)

7 I'm afraid, I ______________ the shopping yet. (not, do)

8 When ______________ they ______________ the disco? (leave)

5 **Einfaches Präsens (einfache Gegenwart) oder Verlaufsform Präsens (Verlaufsform Gegenwart)? Wählen Sie die richtige Zeitform.**

1 I ______________ in a hotel this week. (stay)

2 She always ______________ the bus to work in the morning. (take)

3 They ______________ going out in the evening. (not, like)

4 She ______________ very well today. I don't think she'll win. (not, play)

5 Most people ______________ in the city centre. (work)

6 ______________ you ______________ to football matches? (go, often)

6 **Machen Sie ein Häkchen neben die Sätze, die als Voraussagen zu betrachten sind.**

1 It's only half past five. We won't be late.

2 It's raining outside. I'll get my umbrella.

3 It's very cloudy now. I'm sure it'll rain this evening.

4 Have you met my brother? I'll introduce you to him.

5 My car is at the garage so we'll get the bus to the station.

6 Are you going to the concert? You'll really enjoy it.

7 **Schreiben Sie Sätze über sich. Verwenden Sie dabei die folgenden Ausdrücke der Zeit.**

1 at the moment

____

2 last Saturday

____

3 tomorrow

____

4 never

____

5 every evening

____

WRITING

Stellen Sie sich vor, Sie nehmen an einem Englischkurs in Großbritannien teil. Schreiben Sie einen Brief an einen Freund oder eine Freundin. Sprechen Sie die folgenden Themen an.

your feelings when you arrived
where you are living   the school
your progress in English   who you have met
what you have seen   where you have been
your feelings now   your plans for the future

____

____

____

____

____

____

____

____

____

____

____

____

____

____

____

____

____

____

____

Grammatikanhang

INHALTSVERZEICHNIS

Present simple
Einfaches Präsens (Einfache Gegenwart)
Formen

Die verkürzte Form wird im gesprochenen Englisch sowie in Privatbriefen verwendet.

Be

Bejahte Form	**Verneinte Form**
I'm (I am)	I'm not (am not)
you we're (are) they	you we aren't (are not) they
he she's (is) it	he she isn't (is not) it

Fragesätze	**Kurze Antworten**
Am I?	Yes, I am. No, I'm not.
Are you/we/they?	Yes, you/we/they are. No, you/we/they're not.
Is he/she/it?	Yes, he/she/it is. No, he/she/it isn't.

Have

Bejahte Form	**Verneinte Form**
I you have we they	I you haven't (have not) we they
he she has it	he she hasn't it

Fragesätze	**Kurze Antworten**
Have I/you/we/they?	Yes, I/you/we/they have. No, I/you/we/they haven't.
Has he/she/it?	Yes, he/she/it has. No, he/she/it hasn't.

Regelmäßige Verben

Bejahte Form	Verneinte Form
I you work we they	I you don't (do not) work we they
he she works it	he she doesn't (does not) work it

Fragesätze	Kurze Antworten
Do I/you/we/they work?	Yes, I/you/we/they do. No, I/you/we/they don't (do not).
Does he/she/it work?	Yes, he/she/it does. No, he/she/it doesn't (does not).

Fragewörter mit *is/are*

What's your name? Where are your parents?

Fragewörter mit *does/do*

Where does he live? What do you do?

Einfaches Präsens: 3. Person Singular

Bei den meisten Verben wird *-s* angefügt.
takes, gets
Bei *do* und *go* und bei Verben mit den Endungen *-ch, -ss, -sh* und *-x* wird *-es* angefügt.
does, goes, watches, finishes
Bei Verben mit der Endung *-y* wird das *y* durch *-ies* ersetzt.
carries, tries

Gebrauch des einfachen Präsens

- Man beschreibt mit dem einfachen Präsens Bräuche. (Siehe Lektion 7)
  In Spain people have dinner at ten or eleven in the evening.
  In Britain people leave work at five in the afternoon.
- Das einfache Präsens beschreibt regelmäßig wiederkehrende Vorgänge und Handlungen. (Siehe Lektion 9)
  I go running every day.
  We see friends at the weekend.
- Man benutzt das einfache Präsens um zu beschreiben, wie oft man eine Sache macht. (Siehe Lektion 11)
  I always get up at seven o'clock.
  I sometimes do the shopping in the evening.
- Man benutzt das einfache Präsens, um eine Sache zu beschreiben, die langfristig besteht. (Siehe Lektion 25)
  He wears glasses.

Present continuous

Verlausform Präsens (Verlaufsform Gegenwart)

Formen

Die Verlaufsform Präsens bildet man mit *be* + Partizip Präsens (*-ing*). Die verkürzte Form wird im gesprochenen Englisch sowie in Privatbriefen verwendet.

Bejahte Form	Verneinte Form
I'm (am) working	I'm not (am not) working
you we're (are) working they	you we aren't (are not) working they
he she's (is) working it	he she isn't (is not) working it

Fragesätze	Kurze Antworten
Am I working?	Yes, I am. No, I'm not.
Are you/we/they working?	Yes, you/we/they are. No, you/we/they aren't.
Is he/she/it working?	Yes, he/she it is. No, he/she/it isn't.

Fragewörter

What are you doing? Why are you laughing?

Partizip Präsens (*-ing*)-Endungen (Verlaufsform)

Bei den meisten Verben wird das Partizip Präsens mit Anfügen von *-ing* gebildet:
go - going visit - visiting

Bei Verben mit stummem End *-e* entfällt das *e*. *-ing* wird angefügt.
make - making have - having

Bei einsilbigen Verben mit der Endung Vokal + Konsonant wird der Endkonsonant verdoppelt und *-ing* angefügt.
get - getting shop - shopping

Bei Verben mit einem Endvokal oder mit der Endung *-y* oder *-w* wird *-ing* angefügt.
draw - drawing play - playing

Folgende Verben werden meistens nicht in der Verlaufsform Präsens verwendet:
believe, feel, hate, hear, know, like, love, see, smell, sound, taste, think, understand, want

Gebrauch der Verlaufsform Präsens

- Mit der Verlaufsform Präsens beschreibt man etwas, was zum Zeitpunkt des Sprechens geschieht bzw. etwas, was noch nicht aber bald abgeschlossen wird. (Siehe Lektion 15 und 23)
  We're flying at 10.000 meters.
  She's wearing a yellow dress.
- Mit der Verlaufsform Präsens beschreibt man einen Plan oder ein Vorhaben, das ziemlich sicher ist. (Siehe Lektion 24)
  We're going to see Mary on Saturday.
  He's coming round this evening.

Past simple
Einfaches Präteritum (Einfache Vergangenheit)

Formen

Die verkürzte Form wird im gesprochenen Englisch und in Privatbriefen verwendet.

Be

Bejahte Form		Verneinte Form	
I		I	
he	was	he	wasn't (was not)
she		she	
it		it	
you		you	
we	were	we	weren't (were not)
they		they	

Have

Bejahte Form		Verneinte Form	
I		I	
you		you	
we		we	
they	had	they	didn't (did not) have
he		he	
she		she	
it		it	

Regelmäßige Verben

Bejahte Form		Verneinte Form	
I		I	
you		you	
we		we	
they	worked	they	didn't (did not) work
he		he	
she		she	
it		it	

Fragesätze	Kurze Antworten
Did I/you/we/they work ?	Yes, I/you/we/they did.
Did he/she/it work?	Yes, he/she/it did.
	No, I/you/we/they didn't.
	No, he/she/it didn't.

Fragewörter

What did you do yesterday? Why did you leave?

Endungen beim einfachen Präteritum

Bei den meisten regelmäßigen Verben wird *-ed* angefügt.
walk - walked watch - watched

Bei Verben mit End *-e* wird *-d* angefügt.
close - closed continue - continued

Bei einsilbigen Verben mit der Endung Vokal + Konsonant wird der Endkonsonant verdoppelt und *-ed* angefügt.
stop - stopped plan - planned

Bei Verben mit der Endung *-y* wird das *y* durch *-ied* ersetzt.
study - studied try - tried

Bei Verben mit der Endung Vokal + *-y* wird *-ed* angefügt.
play - played annoy - annoyed

Unregelmäßige Verben

Es gibt viele Verben mit einer unregelmäßigen Form beim einfachen Präteritum. Eine Liste der in **Reward Elementary** vorkommenden unregelmäßigen Verben erscheint auf Seite 92.

Aussprache von Endungen beim einfachen Präteritum

/t/ *finished, liked, walked*
/d/ *continued, lived, stayed*
/ɪd/ *decided, started, visited*

Zeitangaben der Vergangenheit

(Siehe Lektion 22)
yesterday morning/afternoon/evening
last Saturday/week/month/year
two weeks ago/six months ago

Gebrauch des einfachen Präteritums

- Mit dem einfachen Präteritum beschreibt man Handlungen oder Ereignisse, die vergangen sind und die als abgeschlossen gelten. (Siehe Lektion 16, 18, 20 und 22)
  What were you like as a child?
  I started learning English last year.
  Did they go to France last year?

Future simple (*will*)

Einfaches Futur (Einfache Zukunft)

Formen

Das einfache Futur wird gebildet mit *will* + Grundform des Verbs. Die verkürzte Form wird im gesprochenen Englisch sowie in Privatbriefen verwendet.

Bejahte Form		Verneinte Form	
I		I	
you		you	
we		we	
they	'll (will) work	they	won't (will not) work
he		he	
she		she	
it		it	

Fragesätze	Kurze Antworten
Will I/you/we/they work?	Yes, I/you/we/they will.
he/she/it/	he/she/it/
	No, I/you/we/they won't.
	he/she/it

Fragewörter

What will you do? *Where will you go?*

Gebrauch des einfachen Futurs

- Mit dem einfachen Futur spricht man spontan gefasste Entscheidungen aus. (Siehe Lektion 26 und 36)
  I'll have the blue T-shirt.
  I think I'll go out tonight.
  I'll call back later.
- Mit dem einfachen Futur macht man Vorhersagen oder Meinungsäußerungen über zukünftige Ereignisse. (Siehe Lektion 37)
  There'll be more and more people in the world.
  I think it'll be hot tomorrow.

Present perfect simple

Einfaches Perfekt (Einfache Vollendete Gegenwart)

Formen

Das einfache Perfekt bildet man mit *has/have* + Partizip Perfekt. Die verkürzte Form wird im gesprochenen Englisch sowie in Privatbriefen verwendet.

Bejahte Form		Verneinte Form	
I		I	
you	've (have) worked	you	haven't (have not) worked
we		we	
they		they	
he		he	
she	's (has) worked	she	hasn't (has not) worked
it		it	

Fragesätze	Kurze Antworten
Have I/you/we/they worked?	Yes, I/you/we/they have.
	No, I/you/we/they haven't.
Has he/she/it worked ?	Yes, he/she/it has.
	No, he/she/it hasn't.

Partizip Perfekt

Das Partizip Perfekt von allen regelmäßigen sowie von manchen unregelmäßigen Verben gleicht der Form beim einfachen Präteritum.

Regelmäßig *move - moved, finish - finished, visit - visited*
Unregelmäßig *leave - left, find - found, buy - bought*

Das Partizip Perfekt von manchen unregelmäßigen Verben gleicht nicht der Form des einfachen Präteritums.

go - went - gone *be - was/were - been*
drink - drank - drunk *ring - rang - rung*

Eine Liste der in **Reward Elementary** vorkommenden unregelmäßigen Verben erscheint auf Seite 92.

Been und *gone*

He's been to America. = *He's been there and he's back here now.*
He's gone to America. = *He's still there.*

Gebrauch des einfachen Perfekts

- Das einfache Perfekt beschreibt Erfahrungen. Man benutzt diese Form oft im Zusammenhang mit *ever* und *never*. (Siehe Lektion 32)
  Have you ever stayed in a hotel? (=Do you have the experience of staying in a hotel?)
  Yes, I have. (=Yes I have stayed in a hotel at some point but it's not important when.)
  No, I've never stayed in a hotel.

  Beachten Sie: Wenn weitere Informationen über diese Erfahrungen oder Handlungen gegeben werden und dabei *when, how, why* oder *how long* stehen, muss das einfache Präteritum angewendet werden.
  When did you stay in a hotel? - When I was in France last year.

- Mit dem einfachen Perfekt beschreibt man Ereignisse in der Vergangenheit, die eine Wirkung auf die Gegenwart haben. Man beschreibt damit oft Veränderungen. (Siehe Lektion 33)
  He's hurt his back.
  He's lost his wallet.

  Man verwendet *just* bei der Beschreibung von Handlungen, die gerade erst abgeschlossen wurden.
  He's just lost his wallet.

  Man verwendet *yet* bei Fragen und verneinten Form im Zusammenhang mit Handlungen, die erwartet werden. Das Wort *yet* erscheint meistens am Satzende.
  Have you been to the doctor yet?

  Bei der Beschreibung, wann ein einmaliges, bestimmtes Ereignis stattgefunden hat, wird das einfache Präteritum verwendet.
  He hurt his back this morning.

Questions

Fragesätze

Es gibt zwei Möglichkeiten, Fragesätze zu bilden:

- Ohne ein Fragewort. (Siehe Lektion 3)
  Are you British?
  Was he born in Italy?
  Do you have any brothers?
  Did you get up late this morning?

- Mit einem Fragewort wie z.B. *who, what, where, when, how, why*. (Siehe Lektion 9)
  What's his job?
  How old is he?
  What do you do to relax?
  Where were you born?

Nach *what* und *which* kann man ein Substantiv (Hauptwort) verwenden.
What time is it?
Which road will you take?

Nach *how* kann man ein Adjektiv (Eigenschaftswort) oder ein Adverb (Umstandswort) verwenden.
How much is it?
How long does it take by car?
How fast can you drive?

Who, what oder *which* können als Fragepronomen in Bezug auf den Satzgegenstand verwendet werden. Man verwendet dabei weder *do* noch *did*.
What's your first name?
Who was Agatha Christie?

Who, what oder *which* können als Fragepronomen in Bezug auf das Satzobjekt verwendet werden. In diesem Fall muss *do* oder *did* verwendet werden.
What did Agatha Christie do?
Who did she marry?

Etwas indirektere, höflichere Fragesätze kann man mit den folgenden Frageausdrücken bilden:
Can I help you?
Could I have some water please?
Would you like a regular or a large Coke?

Imperatives

Imperativ (Befehlsform)

Der Imperativ hat die gleiche Form wie die Grundform des Verbs (ohne *to*) und hat meistens keinen Satzgegenstand.

Gebrauch des Imperativs

- Mit dem Imperativ zeigt man jemandem den Weg. (Siehe Lektion 14)
  Go along East Street.
  Turn left into Prince Street.

- Mit dem Imperativ gibt man Anweisungen und Ratschläge. (Siehe Lektion 34)
  Come in.
  Sit down.
  Check the weather forecast before you go.

Eine negative Anweisung wird mit *don't* + Grundform des Verbs gebildet.
Don't take too much to carry.

Verb patterns
Verbmuster

Bei gewissen Verben gibt es verschiedene Möglichkeiten der Satzkonstruktion: Entweder die *ing*- Form oder die Grundform des Verbs mit oder ohne *to*.

ing-Form

Nach gewissen Verben kann man die *ing*-Form eines Verbs verwenden. (Siehe Lektion 10)
I like playing football on the beach.
Peter hates travelling by plane.

Beachten Sie dabei, dass sich *would like to do something* auf ein Ereignis bezieht, das zu einem bestimmten Zeitpunkt in der Zukunft stattfinden soll.
I'd like to go to the cinema next Saturday.

Der Begriff *like doing something* bezieht sich auf eine Sache, die man immer gern macht.
I like going to the cinema. I go most weekends.

to + Grundform des Verbs

Man kann *to* + Grundform des Verbs nach vielen Verben verwenden. Hier eine Auswahl solcher Verben:
decide go have hope learn like need want
He decided to go to Spain for a holiday.

Gebrauch von *to* + Grundform des Verbs

- Mit *to* + Grundform des Verbs erklärt man, warum man etwas macht. (Siehe Lektion 34)
  You go to a chemist to buy suncream.
  You go to the bus stop to catch a bus.
- Mit *to* + Grundform des Verbs beschreibt man den Zweck einer Sache. (Siehe Lektion 34)
  You use ice to keep things cold.

Have got

Formen
Die verkürzte Form wird im gesprochenen Englisch sowie in Privatbriefen verwendet.

Bejahte Form		Verneinte Form	
I you we they	've (have) got	I you we they	haven't (have not) got
he she it	's (has) got	he she it	hasn't (has not) got

Frage	Kurze Antworten
Have I/you/we/they got ?	Yes, I/you/we/they have. No, I/you/we/they haven't.
Has he/she/it got ?	Yes, he/she/it has. No, he/she/it hasn't.

Gebrauch von *have got*
Man beschreibt mit *have got* Besitzverhältnisse.
He's got a new car.
Have got hat die gleiche Bedeutung wie *have*. Man verwendet *have got* im gesprochenen Englisch sowie in Privatbriefen.
She's got a house in London. (= She has a house in London.)

Going to

Gebrauch von *going to* + Grundform des Verbs

- Man verwendet *going to* + Grundform des Verbs, um eine Absicht oder einen bereits gefassten Plan zu beschreiben. (Siehe Lektion 24)
  I'm going to see my friends more often.
- Man verwendet *going to* + Grundform des Verbs, um ein zukünftiges Ereignis zu beschreiben, das zum Zeitpunkt der Äußerung gewiss ist. (Siehe Lektion 24)
  She's going to have a baby.

Modal Verbs
Modale Hilfsverben

Folgende Verben sind modale Hilfsverben:
can could must should will would needn't

Formen

- Modale Hilfsverben haben die gleiche Form in allen Personen.
  I must go.
  He must be quiet.
- Bei Fragen und der verneinten Form mit modalen Hilfsverben wird das Hilfsverb *do* nicht verwendet.
  Can you use a computer?
  You mustn't be late for the meeting.
- Nach modalen Hilfsverben wird die Grundform des Verbs ohne *to* verwendet.
  I can type.
  You should see a doctor.

Gebrauch der modalen Hilfsverben

Can

- Mit *can* drückt man Fähigkeit und Können aus. Man beschreibt etwas, was man fast immer in der Lage ist zu tun. (Siehe Lektion 13)
  I can play the piano.
  I can drive a car.
- Mit *can* bittet man um Erlaubnis. (Siehe Lektion 26)
  Can I try this on?
- Mit *can* gewährt man Erlaubnis. (Siehe Lektion 31)
  You can go to London on Saturday.

Man könnte auch *could* verwenden. *Can* ist etwas weniger formell als *could.*

Could

- Mit *could* bittet man höflich um etwas.
  Could I have some water, please?
- Mit *could* bittet man jemanden um etwas.
  Could you tell me your name?
- Mit *could* bittet man um Erlaubnis.
  Could I try this on?

Must

- Mit *must* drückt man einen dringenden Rat, eine Notwendigkeit und eine Verpflichtung aus. (Siehe Lektion 31)
  You really must stop smoking.
  It's late. I must go now.
  You must stop at a red light.

Must wird oft bei Sicherheitsvorkehrungen verwendet.
You must use your seatbelt.

Mustn't

- Mit *mustn't* gibt man jemandem einen dringenden Rat, was er nicht tun soll. (Siehe Lektion 31)
  You mustn't point at people.
- Man beschreibt mit *mustn't* eine Sache, die man auf keinen Fall machen darf, eine Sache, die allgemein verboten ist. (Siehe Lektion 31)
  You mustn't drive through a red light.

Man könnte auch *can't* verwenden.
You can't drive through a red light.

Bei Fragesätzen wird *must* meistens nicht verwendet.

Should

- Mit *should* gibt man einen Rat, oder man macht Vorschläge. Man drückt mit *should* seine Meinung aus. (Siehe Lektion 28)
  You should go to bed.
  You shouldn't go to work.

Will

siehe einfaches Futur (einfache Zukunft): *will*

Would like + Substantiv bzw. *would like* + Grundform des Verbs

- Mit *would like* + Substantiv bzw. *would like* + Grundform des Verbs bietet oder fordert man etwas höflich an. (Siehe Lektion 25)
  Would you like a drink?
  What would you like to drink.
  I'd like a burger, please.
  I'd like to go to the cinema tonight.
- Man verwendet *like* allein, um eine Sache zu beschreiben, die man immer mag.
  I like Coke. (= immer)
  I'd like a Coke. (= jetzt)

Needn't

Mit *needn't* beschreibt man eine Handlung, die nicht notwendig ist.
You needn't do your homework tonight.

Pronouns

Pronomen (Fürwörter)

Subjekt (Satzgegenstand) (Siehe Lektion 10)	**Objekt** (Satzergänzung) (Siehe Lektion 10)	**Possessivpronomen** (persönliches Fürwort) (Siehe Lektion 27)
I	me	mine
you	you	yours
he	him	his
she	her	hers
it	it	ist
we	us	ours
they	them	theirs

Articles

Artikel

Es gibt viele Regeln bei der Verwendung von Artikeln. Es folgen die nützlichsten Regeln. (Siehe Lektion 2 und 12)

Gebrauch des unbestimmten Artikels *a/an*

- Mit dem unbestimmten Artikel spricht man über eine Sache zum ersten Mal.
  She works in an office in Paris.
  I get a train to work.
- Man verwendet den unbestimmten Artikel bei Berufsbezeichnungen.
  She's a marketing consultant.
  He's a ticket inspector.
- Man verwendet den unbestimmten Artikel bei gewissen Mengenangaben.
  I go to the cinema once or twice a month.
  There are several trains a day.

an wird vor Vokalen verwendet:
an accountant
an apple

Gebrauch des bestimmten Artikels *the*

- Man verwendet *the*, wenn man weiter über eine bereits erwähnte Sache spricht.
  The office is near the Gare du Nord.
  I get the eight o'clock train.
- Mit *the* beschreibt man eine Sache, die es nur einmal gibt.
  The Channel Tunnel.
  The Eurostar service.

Vor Vokalen wird *the* /ði:/ ausgesprochen.

Kein Artikel

- Gewisse Ausdrücke werden ohne Artikel angewendet.
  by train *by plane* *at work* *at home*
- Bei den Namen der meisten Ländern, bei Mahlzeiten und bei Sprachen verwendet man keinen Artikel.
  She often goes to France.
  She lives in Britain.
  Let's have lunch.
  I speak Italian.

Plurals

Plural-Nomen (Plural-Substantive)

Die Plural-Form von Nomen (Substantiven) wird in der Regel durch Anhängen von *-s* gebildet. (Siehe Lektion 4 und 6)
bag - bags *book - books* *key - keys*

Bei der Pluralbildung von Substantiven mit der Endung *-y* wird das *y* durch *-ies* ersetzt.
diary - diaries *baby - babies*

Die Plural-Form von Substantiven mit den Endungen *-o, -ch, -ss, -sh* und *-x* wird durch Anhängen von *-es* gebildet.
watch - watches *glass - glasses*

Es gibt auch unregelmäßige Plural-Formen.
man - men *woman - women* *child - children*

Possessives

Possessiv-Formen (Besitzanzeigende Formen)

Possessiv 's

Im Singular wird *'s* an das Nomen (Substantiv) angefügt. (Siehe Lektion 6)
John's mother.
His teacher's book.

Bei Substantiven mit regelmäßiger Pluralbildung wird *s'* angefügt.
My parents' names are Georges and Paulette.
The boys' room.

Bei Substantiven mit unregelmäßger Pluralbildung wird *'s* angefügt.
Their children's names are Pierre and Thierry.
The men's room.

Possessiv-Adjektive

Die wichtigsten Anwendungen für Possessiv-Adjektive werden in Lektion 2 aufgelistet.

Formen

I	you	he	she	it	we	they
my	your	his	her	its	our	their

Whose

Man verwendet *whose* bei der Frage, wem eine Sache gehört. (Siehe Lektion 27)
Whose bag is this?
Whose are these shoes?

Expressions of quantity

Mengenangaben

Zählbare und nicht zählbare Nomen (Substantive)

Zählbare Substantive haben sowohl eine Singular-Form als auch eine Plural-Form. (Siehe Lektion 17)
a banana - bananas, a tomato - tomatoes

Nicht zählbare Substantive haben normalerweise keine Plural-Form.
water, juice, wine

Bei der Beschreibung von verschiedenen Sorten von nicht zählbaren Substantiven werden diese zählbar.
Beaujolais and Bordeaux are both French wines.

Some und *any*

Man verwendet *some* bei Plural-Substantiven sowie bei nicht zählbaren Substantiven in der bejahten Form, um eine nicht bestimmte Menge anzuzeigen. (Siehe Lektion 8 und 17)
We need some fruit and vegetables.

Man verwendet *any* bei Plural-Substantiven sowie bei nicht zählbaren Substantiven in verneinten Sätzen und bei Fragen. (Siehe Lektion 8 und 17)
We haven't got any carrots.
Have we got any milk?

Man verwendet *some* in Fragen, bei denen es sich um Bitten, Angebote oder Vorschläge handelt.
How about some oranges?

Adjectives

Adjektive

Stellung von Adjektiven

Es gibt zwei mögliche Stellungen von Adjektiven. (Siehe Lektion 4)

- Nach dem Verb *to be*
  The book is very interesting
- Vor einem Nomen (Substantiv)
  It's an interesting book.

Steigerungsformen - Komparativ und Superlativ

Formen

Bei den meisten Adjektiven wird *-er* angefügt, um die Komparativ-Form zu bilden und *-est* angefügt, um die Superlativ-Form zu bilden. (Siehe Lektion 29 und 30)
cold - colder - coldest *cheap - cheaper - cheapest*

Bei Adjektiven mit der Endung *-e* wird *-r* angefügt, um die Komparativ-Form zu bilden und *-st* angefügt, um die Superlativ-Form zu bilden.
large - larger - largest *fine - finer - finest*

Bei Adjektiven mit der Endung *-y* wird das y durch *-ier* ersetzt, um die Komparativ-Form zu bilden und durch *-iest* ersetzt, um die Superlativ-Form zu bilden.
happy - happier - happiest *friendly - friendlier - friendliest*

Bei einsilbigen Adjektiven mit der Endung Vokal + Konsonant wird der Endkonsonant verdoppelt und *-er* zur Bildung der Komparativ-Form oder *-est* zur Bildung der Superlativ-Form angefügt.
hot - hotter - hottest *thin - thinner - thinnest*

Bei längeren Adjektiven wird die Komparativ-Form mit *more* gebildet und die Superlativ-Form mit *most.*
expensive - more expensive - most expensive
important - more important - most important

Es gibt auch unregelmäßige Steigerungsformen.
good - better - best *bad - worse - worst*

Bei der Superlativ-Form wird *the* vor dem Adjektiv verwendet.
James ist the tallest person in the room.

Beim Vergleich von zwei verschiedenen Sachen wird die Komparativ-Form + *than* verwendet.
Thailand is bigger than Britain.

Adverbs

Adverbien (Umstandswörter)

Bildung von Adverbien

Mit einem Adverb beschreibt man ein Verb. (Siehe Lektion 35)
She speaks English fluently.
He drives carelessly.

Man bildet ein Adverb, indem man *-ly* an das Adjektiv anfügt.
fluent - fluently *careless - carelessly*

Bei Adjektiven mit der Endung *-y* wird das *y* durch *-ily* ersetzt.
happy - happily *easy - easily*

Manche Adverbien haben die gleiche Form wie beim Stamm-Adjektiv.
late, early, hard

Das Adverb zu *good* heißt *well.*
She's a good writer.
She writes well.

Stellung von Adverbien der Häufigkeit

Adverbien der Häufigkeit stehen unmittelbar vor dem Verb. (Siehe Lektion 11)
I always get up at seven o'clock.
I often have a drink with friends.

Beim Verb *to be* folgt das Adverb immer dem Verb.
I'm never late for work.

Prepositions of time and place

Präpositionen (Verhältniswörter) der Zeit und des Ortes

in, at, on, to

Gebrauch von *in*

- Man verwendet *in* im Zusammenhang mit Jahreszeiten und Monaten.
  in winter, in September, in March
- Man verwendet *in* bei Ortsangaben. (Siehe Lektion 5)
  in the classroom, in the photograph, in Greece
- Man verwendet *in* im Zusammenhang mit manchen Tageszeiten. (Siehe Lektion 7)
  in the morning, in the afternoon

Gebrauch von *at*

- Man verwendet *at* im Zusammenhang mit gewissen Ausdrücken. (Siehe Lektion 11)
  at school, at home, at work
- Man verwendet *at* im Zusammenhang mit manchen Tageszeiten. (Siehe Lektion 11)
  at night, at seven o'clock, at the weekend

Gebrauch von *on*

- Man verwendet *on* im Zusammenhang mit Wochentagen und bei der Datumsangabe. (Siehe Lektion 11)
  on Sunday, on Monday morning, on 15th June

Gebrauch von *to*

- Man verwendet *to* im Zusammenhang mit Ortsangaben.
  Helena goes to London every month.

Gebrauch von *from ... to*

- Man verwendet *from ... to* bei der Angabe der Dauer. (Siehe Lektion 11)
  The shop is open from seven to nine o'clock.

Present simple passive

Passivform im Einfachen Präsens (Passivform der Einfachen Gegenwart)

Man bildet die Passivform des einfachen Präsens mit *am/is/are* + Partizip Perfekt. (Siehe Lektion 38)
Fiat cars are made in Italy.

Gebrauch der Passivform des einfachen Präsens

Man verwendet die Passivform des einfachen Präsens, um das Satzobjekt zu betonen.
The palace was built by Palladio in 1635.

Reported speech

Indirekte Rede

Man berichtet, was jemand sagt bzw. gesagt hat unter Anwendung von *said that* + Nebensatz. Wenn man direkte Rede zu indirekter Rede umformt, gibt es eine Verschiebung der Zeiten.

Direkte Rede	Indirekte Rede
'The film finishes at ten o'clock,' she said.	*She said the film finished at ten o'clock.*
'We're going on holiday next year,' she said.	*She said they were going on holiday next year.*
'We'll catch the train to Paris,' he said.	*He said they would catch the train to Paris.*
'I watched the television all evening,' he said.	*He said he had watched the television all evening.*

Unregelmäßige Verben

Verben mit der gleichen Form im Infinitiv, der einfachen Vergangenheit und des Partizip Perfekt

cost	cost	cost
cut	cut	cut
hit	hit	hit
let	let	let
put	put	put
read /ri:d/	read /red/	read /red/
set	set	set
shut	shut	shut

Verben mit der gleichen Form in der einfachen Vergangenheit und dem Partizip Perfekt, aber mit einem anderen Infinitiv

bring	brought	brought
build	built	built
burn	burnt/burned	burnt/burned
buy	bought	bought
catch	caught	caught
feel	felt	felt
find	found	found
get	got	got
have	had	had
hear	heard	heard
hold	held	held
keep	kept	kept
learn	learnt/learned	learnt/learned
leave	left	left
lend	lent	lent
light	lit/lighted	lit/lighted
lose	lost	lost
make	made	made
mean	meant	meant
meet	met	met
pay	paid	paid
say	said	said
sell	sold	sold
send	sent	sent
sit	sat	sat
sleep	slept	slept
smell	smelt/smelled	smelt/smelled
spell	spelt/spelled	spelt/spelled
spend	spent	spent
stand	stood	stood
teach	taught	taught
understand	understood	understood
win	won	won

Verben mit der gleichen Form im Infinitiv und im Partizip Perfekt, aber mit einer anderen Form in der einfachen Vergangenheit

become	became	become
come	came	come
run	ran	run

Verben mit verschiedenen Formen im Infinitiv, der einfachen Vergangenheit und des Partizip Perfekt

be	was/were	been
begin	began	begun
break	broke	broken
choose	chose	chosen
do	did	done
draw	drew	drawn
drink	drank	drunk
drive	drove	driven
eat	ate	eaten
fall	fell	fallen
fly	flew	flown
forget	forgot	forgotten
give	gave	given
go	went	gone
grow	grew	grown
know	knew	known
lie	lay	lain
ring	rang	rung
rise	rose	risen
see	saw	seen
show	showed	shown
sing	sang	sung
speak	spoke	spoken
swim	swam	swum
take	took	taken
throw	threw	thrown
wake	woke	woken
wear	wore	worn
write	wrote	written

Aussprache

/ɑː/	park
/æ/	hat
/aɪ/	my
/aʊ/	how
/e/	ten
/eɪ/	bay
/eə/	there
/ɪ/	sit
/iː/	me
/ɪə/	beer
/ɒ/	what
/əʊ/	no
/ɔː/	more
/ɔɪ/	toy
/ʊ/	took
/uː/	soon
/ʊə/	tour
/ɜː/	sir
/ʌ/	sun
/ə/	better

/b/	buy
/d/	day
/f/	free
/g/	give
/h/	house
/j/	you
/k/	cat
/l/	look
/m/	mean
/n/	nice
/p/	paper
/r/	rain
/s/	sad
/t/	time
/v/	verb
/w/	wine
/z/	zoo
/ʃ/	shirt
/ʒ/	leisure
/ŋ/	sing
/tʃ/	church
/θ/	thank
/ð/	then
/dʒ/	jacket

Tapescripts

Lesson 1 Sounds, activity 1

Japan China Canada Korea Germany
Russia Brazil Turkey Ukraine Morocco

Lesson 1 Listening, activity 1

Conversation 1

JUAN Hello, I'm Juan.
ANNA Hello, Juan. My name's Anna. I'm from France. Where are you from, Juan?
JUAN I'm from Barcelona in Spain.

Conversation 2

MR THOMAS Hello, my name's Thomas, Peter Thomas.
MR PLACIDI Hello, Mr Thomas. I'm Marco Placidi. I'm from Naples in Italy. Where are you from?
MR THOMAS I'm from Philadelphia in the United States of America.

Conversation 3

INGRID Hello, I'm Ingrid. What's your name?
SALLY Hello, Ingrid. My name's Sally. Where are you from?
INGRID I'm from Sweden. And you, Sally? Where are you from?
SALLY I'm from Toronto in Canada.

Conversation 4

JANET SMITH Hello, my name's Janet Smith.
MARILYN KELLY Hello, Mrs Smith. I'm Marilyn Kelly.
JANET SMITH Where are you from, Mrs Kelly?
MARILYN KELLY I'm from Sydney in Australia.

Lesson 2 Listening, activity 1

JAN Hi there. My name's Jan. I'm from America. I'm a secretary here at the university.
LEE Hello, Jan. My name's Lee. I'm from Buenos Aires in Argentina. I'm a teacher.
JAN This is my friend, Sara. She's from Canada. She's a student.
LEE Hello, Sara.
SARA Hello, Lee.

Lesson 2 Listening, activity 2

A Hello, Peter. What's your friend's name?
B His name's Silvio.
A Where's he from?
B He's from Italy.
A What's his job?
B He's an accountant.

Lesson 3 Sounds

1 Where are you from?
2 How old are you?
3 What is your address?
4 Who is your favourite actor?
5 Where is your home?
6 What is your telephone number

Lesson 3 Listening, activity 1

INTERVIEWER Hello.
MARIA Hello.
INTERVIEWER I'm Sheila Grange. I'm the hotel manager. Please sit down. Now, what is your name?
MARIA My name is Maria Verde.
INTERVIEWER You are interested in a job here at the Continental Hotel. Is that right?
MARIA Yes, that's right.
INTERVIEWER What's your job now?
MARIA I'm a receptionist at the Hilton in London.
INTERVIEWER How old are you Miss Verde?
MARIA I'm twenty-five years old.
INTERVIEWER Are you married?
MARIA No, I'm single.
INTERVIEWER Are you British?
MARIA No, I'm Italian. I'm from Milan.
INTERVIEWER Your English is excellent!
MARIA Thank you.

Lesson 4 Grammar and Sounds, activity 1

43 13 97 56 51 12 63 17 8 94
77 15 85 3 39

Lesson 4 Grammar and Sounds, activity 2

classrooms teachers addresses numbers
colleges classes chairs

Lesson 5 Sounds, activity 1

1 WALLET 2 COLOUR 3 COMB
4 CAMERA 5 WATCH 6 DIARY

Lesson 5 Listening

A Where are my glasses ?
B What colour are they?
A Blue and green. They're not in my bag.
B Well, they're not on the table. Are they under your book?
A Oh, yes. Here they are. Thanks.

Lesson 6 Listening, activity 1

SPEAKER 1 We're a very big family. I 'm very lucky, I suppose. I live alone now. My husband's dead. But my children have got houses near here. My daughter is a teacher here in the town and I see her at weekends. She's married. Her husband, Greg, is American. He's very nice and kind. He's got a job with a computer company. They've got a two-year-old daughter, Philippa. I've got three sons. Kevin and Josh are both married with children. Henry is still single. He's a medical student at university.
SPEAKER 2 I'm twenty-eight and I live in Britain now. I've got a good job here. My family are all in the States so I don't see them much. I'm married and we've got a beautiful daughter. Her name is Philippa. My wife, Sally, has got three brothers. Her father's dead and her mother lives near us. She's not very independent, though. Always at our home. She helps Sally look after our daughter. She's a wonderful grandmother and Philippa loves her.

Lesson 7 Sounds, activity 3

1 3.30 **2** 10.15 **3** 7.45 **4** 2.10 **5** 9. 55
6 1.35 **7** 11.30 **8** 7.00 **9** 4.05 **10** 6.40

Lesson 8 Listening, activity 1

SPEAKER 1 My favourite room is a small study where I work in the evenings. It's upstairs next to the bathroom at the back of the house so there is no noise from the road. There are bookcases on two walls of the room and a big desk in front of the window. My computer is on the desk. On one wall there's a big mirror and next to it there's an old armchair that I like very much. It's not a beautiful room but it's a very comfortable room.
SPEAKER 2 I live in a very big house with lots of rooms. The room I like best is a big sitting room at the back of the house. It is a pretty room with some beautiful old furniture. There's a big window with a beautiful view of the garden. There is a comfortable sofa in front of the fire where I sit in the evenings with my family. There are pretty green curtains in front of the window and an old piano next to it. The television and video are on a cupboard near the fire.
SPEAKER 3 My favourite room is my bedroom. It's upstairs at the front of the house. There's a view of the front garden and the town in the distance. In the room there's a bed and next to the bed there's a small table with a lamp. There's a big cupboard next to the door where I put my clothes. Near the window there's a big table with two chairs. There are some plants and a telephone on the table. It isn't really a beautiful room but it is not noisy and it's very comfortable.

Lesson 9 Listening, activity 1

WOMAN 1 I come home before my husband so I have a cup of tea. I listen to the radio and I make dinner. My husband comes home at about 7 and he watches the sport on TV. He doesn't like cooking. We eat in front of the TV. On Wednesdays I go to a friend's house for the evening. My husband goes to a club with friends or to the cinema.
On Saturday we go to town to the shops in the morning. My husband goes to a football match with friends in the afternoon and I go to a jazz club with my friends. In the evening we go to a restaurant or to a discotheque with friends. On Sundays we get up at midday, have lunch, and work in the house. My husband washes the car and I go running in the park. We watch TV and go to bed early.
WOMAN 2 I come home from work at about 6.30. I read the newspaper and relax. When my husband comes home, we have a drink together then he makes dinner. We eat in front of the television. On Tuesday evenings we go out with friends. We go to the cinema or to a nightclub. On Wednesdays I have a language class and then I have dinner with a friend. I come home at 11.

On Saturdays we go to a supermarket to do the shopping for the week. And in the evening we go out with friends. Most Sundays we go to my parents' house for the afternoon. Some weekends we go to see friends in the country. In the evening I work on the computer.

Lesson 10 Listening, activity 1

Conversation 1

MAN I like this very much. What is it?
WOMAN I don't know. It's modern art. I don't like it at all.
MAN What about that painting near the door? It's very beautiful.
WOMAN No, it isn't. It's horrible! It's just a blue and red mess.
MAN Well, what do you like?
WOMAN I like classical paintings by real artists!
MAN I just like good paintings. Classical and modern.

Conversation 2

WOMAN Do you like the music?
MAN No. What is it?
WOMAN It's reggae. I love it. It's great for dancing. I come here every Saturday evening.
MAN It's very noisy.
WOMAN Do you like dancing?
MAN Well, um, I don't know. You see, this is my first visit to a night club.
WOMAN Well, what music do you like?
MAN I like classical music. I play the violin in an orchestra.
WOMAN I hate classical music. It's no good for dancing.

Lesson 11 Listening, activity 3

MUSICIAN I play in a club on Friday, Saturday and Wednesday evenings. I play the guitar in a rock group. There are four of us. On the nights we play I have a snack at home at 7 o'clock. I leave home at 8 o'clock and I take a taxi to the club. We usually start playing at 9.00 but I always get to the club at 8.15 to get things ready. We sometimes have a drink with the owner of the club. Most people arrive around 9.30. We usually play for an hour and a half, then we have a break. We always have a snack and a drink. We play again from 11.30 to about 1 o'clock. On Tuesday and Thursday mornings I practise with the other musicians.

CHEF I get up at 8.00 most mornings and have a shower and a big breakfast with my wife. My wife leaves for work at 8.45 and I relax and read the newspaper for half an hour. I leave the house at 9.40. The restaurant is near my home so I walk to work. I have lunch in the kitchen at 2 o'clock and then I walk home. My wife works in the mornings and she is usually at the house when I get home. In the afternoon I relax at home or go out to the park with my wife. At six o'clock I go back to work and I get home at 11 o'clock. I don't go to work on Sundays and Mondays.

Lesson 14 Listening, activity 1

Conversation 1

A Excuse me. Where can I get some stamps?
B At the post office.
A Is there a post office near here?
B Yes. Go along Broad Street. Turn right into the High Street, then straight ahead into High Town. The post office is opposite the book shop. It's behind the Old House.
A Thank you very much.

Conversation 2

C Excuse me. Can you tell me where I can buy some aspirin?
D The best place is the chemist's in the High Street.
C Can you tell me where it is, please?
D Yes, of course. Walk along Broad Street. Turn right into the High Street. The chemist's is opposite the newsagent's. It's on the left of a sports shop.
C Thank you very much.

Conversation 3

E Hello, Peter. How are you?
F Fine thanks. Why are you here in town?
E I'm with my parents. We are looking for a nice place to eat. Can you tell me where there is a good Italian restaurant?
F Yes. There's a restaurant called Pasta in Widemarsh Street. It has a good reputation.
E How can I get to Widemarsh Street from here? Is it far?
F No. About five minutes' walk. Go down Broad Street. Turn right into the High Street, then turn left into Widemarsh Street. Go along there for about fifty metres and the restaurant is on the right opposite the baker's. There's a Chinese restaurant on the same side of the road.
E Thanks. Bye.

Lesson 15 Listening, activity 3

Conversation 1

A Bridgeton 319850.
B Hello. Is that you, mother? It's Anna.
A Hello Anna. Where are you phoning from?
B From the hotel. We're staying in a hotel right in the centre of the city. We can see the sea from our bedroom window.
A Are you enjoying yourselves?
B We're having a wonderful time. The city is very attractive and there are lots of interesting things to visit. The port is my favourite place. It's very exciting.
A Is the weather good?
B Not very good. It's raining at the moment. But it isn't cold.
A Well, have a good time, Anna. Phone me when you get home. Bye.
B Bye.

Conversation 2

C Penally 765 316.
D Hi, Jim. It's me, Stephie.
C Hello. How was your flight?
D Great! The plane was on time. No problems at all. Is everything OK at home?
C Fine. The children are in bed. Is it nice? What sort of place is it?
D It's a beautiful place in the mountains. We're staying in a hotel outside the town. It's a big chalet. The town is very small and modern. There's lots of snow for skiing and it's very sunny.
C Are your parents enjoying themselves?
D Oh, yes. They're having a wonderful time. But they're very tired. The journey was quite long. Mother is sleeping at the moment and father is having a drink in the bar. We're going to a restaurant this evening. And tomorrow we're going skiing.
C Well, have a good holiday. See you next week. Bye.
D Bye Jim.

Lesson 16 Vocabulary and Sounds, activity 3

1 Where were you born?
2 What were you like at school?
3 Who was your best friend at school?
4 What were you good at?
5 Were you often in trouble at school?

Lesson 16 Listening, activity 1

A Hello Jenny. You're home! How was your holiday?
B It was great. I was away for a week.
A Where were you?
B On the south coast.
A Who were you with?
B I was with two friends from college.
A Were you in a good hotel?
B Yes, it was all right. It was in the centre and there was a good view of the sea.
A What was the weather like?
B It wasn't very good. It was nice and warm on Monday and Friday and very cold on the other days.
A What about the food? Was that good?
B Yes, it was excellent.

Lesson 17 Grammar and Listening, activity 4

WOMAN I'd like some vegetable soup with bread, please
WAITER I'm afraid we haven't got any soup today, madam. But we've got some potato salad.
WOMAN I don't like salads. I'll have a cheese omelette.
WAITER Cheese omelette. And for the main course?
WOMAN Roast chicken with boiled potatoes.
WAITER I'm sorry, but we haven't got any chicken But you can have a steak. And there is pasta or chips instead of boiled potatoes.
WOMAN All right. A steak and chips. Have you got any wine or is there only water or tea?
WAITER Of course, madam. We've got some good Bulgarian red wine.
WOMAN Haven't you got any white wine?
WAITER Yes. It's German.
WOMAN That's fine. And cheese. I'd like some cheese and an ice cream.
WAITER Do you want any water?
WOMAN Yes, please. A bottle of spring water.

Lesson 18 Listening, activity 2

Conversation 1

WOMAN There's an interesting article about Kevin Costner. He was born in Los

Angeles in 1955.

MAN He's younger than me!

WOMAN And richer! The article says he studied business at the University of California. That's probably why he's rich!

MAN He didn't study acting, then?

WOMAN Yes. He went to drama school after university.

MAN When did he make his first film?

WOMAN In 1981 he appeared in a film for the first time. And in 1982 he directed his first film.

MAN He received an Oscar for *Dances with Wolves* in 1990. The Oscar for the best director.

WOMAN That was a very good film. He also appeared in *The Bodyguard* with Whitney Houston.

MAN That's right. In 1992. It was a good film, too, but it didn't receive any awards.

WOMAN After that he appeared in *Robin Hood*.

MAN The last film he made was *Waterworld*. That was a very expensive film.

Conversation 2

WOMAN What's the name of the American actress who appeared in *Silence of the Lambs* with Anthony Hopkins?

MAN Jodie Foster. It was a very good film. Very frightening.

WOMAN She received an Oscar for it, didn't she?

MAN Yes. The Oscar for the best actress. It was in 1990. She was quite young. She was born in 1962.

WOMAN But it wasn't her first Oscar, was it?.

MAN No. She received the award in 1988 for the film *The Accused*.

WOMAN Did she study drama?

MAN Yes. She went to Yale University.

WOMAN When did she start acting?

MAN Well, I suppose you can say that she started when she was three years old. She appeared in a television advertisement for sun cream! And then she played in *Taxi Driver* with Robert de Niro when she was only 12 years old.

WOMAN Was she the actress in *Maverick*? That was another good film.

MAN That's right. She played with Mel Gibson. She created her own production company in 1991. And she directs films now.

Lesson 19 Listening, activity 1

Description 1

Attention please, attention please. A little boy of about two years old is looking for his parents. He's got short, dark hair. He's wearing a blue sweater, yellow shorts and white trainers. He says his name is Tom and his baby sister's name is Sally. Can the parents of this little boy please come to the information desk near the entrance immediately? Thank you.

Description 2

A Don't you remember her? She was a very small girl, with long dark hair. She was always on her own. I don't think she had many friends at school. She was very hard working and very good at art. I think she lived in the country.

B Yes, I do remember her. She was very quiet and polite. She didn't talk very much. And she sat at the back of the class in the corner.

A That's right. Well I met her yesterday. She is completely different. She's tall and slim. She's got short fair hair and she wears glasses. She talks a lot now. The change is extraordinary. She was wearing very smart clothes. She was very friendly and we talked a lot about our schooldays.

Description 3

This police announcement is for people in the Halifax area. A dangerous man attacked an elderly couple in the street yesterday. He's about twenty-five. He is medium-height and very thin. He's got short, fair hair and a moustache. He is wearing jeans, a green sweater and a black jacket. He is very dangerous. If you see anyone who looks like this, phone the police immediately. Don't speak to the man, just go to the nearest phone and dial 999.

Lesson 22 Listening

MAN By the way, do you remember Janet Finch? She was at school with us.

WOMAN Yes, of course! What about her?

MAN I met her yesterday at the supermarket.

WOMAN Oh, how is she? The last time I saw her was about ten years ago.

MAN She looked very well. She lived in Italy from 1985 to 1988. She was a teacher in Milan.

WOMAN When did she come back to Britain?

MAN Last year. She spent two months in Coventry, then she moved to Cambridge in the spring.

Lesson 23 Listening, activity 2

The first model is wearing a red skirt. It's very short and shiny. She is wearing matching red and green shoes and a pink sweater. Her hair is orange and she's got small, purple John Lennon sunglasses. The general effect is strange but quite exciting. It will probably be a big success with young people.

The second model is wearing a classic outfit. Very suitable for the business woman. Smart but not too formal. She's got attractive grey trousers, a short yellow jacket over a grey and yellow blouse. She's wearing black boots and she's carrying a matching black bag.

The third model is wearing a long, blue evening dress. The dress is open on one side. She's wearing brown shoes and a small pink scarf. She's carrying a matching blue jacket. The general effect is very sophisticated and quite formal.

The last model is wearing a sports outfit. She's got black jeans with orange socks over the bottom of the jeans. She's got a pair of black trainers. She's wearing a green T-shirt with a black motif on the front. She's carrying a black jacket over her shoulder. A very practical outfit.

Lesson 24 Listening, activity 1

A How are you Betty? And how's Chris? Is he still working for that building company?

B No, Chris stopped work last month. He's sixty-five, you know.

A Goodness! So you're both on holiday all the time now! Have you got any plans?

B Well, first, we're going to have a long holiday. Next summer we're going on a two-month trip.

A Where are you going to?

B Central and South America.

A How wonderful! And are you going to stay here in London or are you going to move to the country?

B We're going to stay here. It's our home. All our friends live in London. And there's a lot to do. But we're going to change flats. This one is too big for two. We're going to buy a small flat near the park. But what about you and John? When are you going to stop work?

A Not for another two years, I'm afraid. I'm looking forward to retiring, but John isn't. He enjoys his job so much.

Lesson 25 Reading and Listening, activity 2

Dialogue 1

A Look, there are some seats over there.

B You two go and sit down and I'll get the orders. What would you like?

A I'd like a gin and orange, please.

B Would you like ice with your gin?

A No, thank you.

C And I'd like a Coke, please. No ice.

B Would you like anything to eat?

A No, thanks.

C I'd like a sandwich, please.

Dialogue 2

A Would you like some potatoes with your steak?

B No thanks, but can I have some more beans, please?

A Yes, help yourself. But leave some for your sister.

B Can I get the tomato ketchup?

A Yes, it's in the cupboard. Can you bring me a beer from the kitchen?

B Is there any mustard?

A Yes. It's in the fridge.

Lesson 26 Listening and Functions, activity 1

A Can I help you, sir?

B Yes. I'm looking for a winter coat.

A Are you looking for something fashionable or a classic style?

B I don't really know. Can you show me what you've got?

A Yes, they're over here.

B Can I try this dark blue one on?

A Yes, of course.

B It doesn't fit me. It's too big. Can I try a smaller size?

A I'm afraid we haven't got a size 40 in blue, sir. Would you like to try the dark green one?

B No, green doesn't suit me. This black one is very nice. It fits very well. I'll take it. How much is it?

A £150, sir. It's an excellent quality coat.

B Oh dear. That's very expensive. I think I'll leave it.

Lesson 28 Grammar and Functions, activity 3

MAN Are you all right?
WOMAN No, I don't feel very well.
MAN What's the matter?
WOMAN I feel sick.
MAN Oh dear!
WOMAN And I've got a headache.
MAN Have you got a temperature?
WOMAN I think so. I feel very hot.

Lesson 29 Vocabulary and Sounds, activity 4

1 The average temperature in Thailand in January is 25°C.
2 The highest point in Great Britain is 1,343 metres.
3 The average annual rainfall in the UK is 600 millimetres.
4 The UK covers a land area of 242,429 square kilometres.
5 The maximum speed on motorways in France is 130 kilometres per hour.
6 New York City's coastline is 920 kilometres long.
7 One litre of water weighs 1 kilogram.

Lesson 32 Listening, activity 2

MAN Have you ever been to Switzerland?
WOMAN No. I've never been there. But I'd like to go. What about you? Have you been?
MAN Yes. I have. I went two years ago for a skiing holiday.
WOMAN Was it very beautiful?
MAN Wonderful. Very beautiful mountain scenery. And the chocolate was delicious!
WOMAN I have been to Russia. I've visited Moscow and St Petersburg. They're beautiful cities. I went to Moscow in the winter. It was very cold.
MAN Did you visit Red Square?
WOMAN Yes, of course.
MAN I'd like to go to Australia.
WOMAN It's great. Beautiful weather. And wonderful beaches for surfing. I'd like to live there.
MAN Oh, you've been there, have you?
WOMAN Yes. I went for two weeks last winter to stay with relatives.
MAN Did you see any kangaroos?
WOMAN Yes. But only in a zoo!

Lesson 33 Reading and Listening, activity 2

JAN Hi, Pete!
PETE Oh, hello, Jan. Have you had a good day?
JAN Great! I've been at the office all day and I've met the new director.What about you? You look very tired. What sort of day have you had?
PETE Awful! I've only just finished the housework.
JAN Oh dear. I am sorry.
PETE I'm afraid, I haven't taken the car to the garage yet.
JAN That doesn't matter. I can take it tomorrow.
PETE Are you very hungry? I haven't made dinner yet.
JAN Oh ... Well, have you done any shopping?
PETE I'm sorry, I haven't had time.
JAN Well, how about going out to eat?
PETE That's a great idea!

Lesson 34 Listening, activity 1

Conversation 1

A So, you're going to Africa for your holiday, are you?
B That's right. We're leaving at the weekend.
A Where are you going in Africa?
B To Kenya. We've got a flight to Nairobi.
A Is that where you can see wild animals like elephants and giraffes?
B Yes. That's why we are going to Kenya.
A Great! Have a good time.

Conversation 2

A What time is it, Jim?
B Half past three.
A Oh dear! I'm going to be late.
A Where are you going?
B To the airport.
A What for?
B To meet my sister. Have you forgotten?

Conversation 3

A Hi! When did you get home?
B About ten minutes ago.
A Have you been into town?
B No, I haven't had time.
A Never mind. What time is it now?
B Five o'clock.
A Well, we need some food for this evening. I'll go to the supermarket now.
B And I'll cook dinner!

Conversation 4

A Have you got the tickets for Eurostar yet?
B I didn't have time to get them this morning.
A Have you phoned the station?
B Yes. They are ready. I need to go and get them.
A Well, I can go now if you like.
B Thank you. That would be great. I don't really have time.

Lesson 35 Listening, activity 1

MAN What are you really good at?
WOMAN Not very many things, I'm afraid. I can swim quite well, but not very fast.
MAN Isn't there anything you can do well?
WOMAN Yes. I'm quite a good dancer. I go to dancing lessons once a week.
MAN What type of dancing?
WOMAN Modern dancing. It's wonderful.
MAN Is there anything you do really badly?
WOMAN Lots of things. I'm a terrible cook. I don't like cooking. I always buy pre-cooked food. I can't sing. I'm also a very bad driver. I go too fast in town and too slowly on the motorway.
MAN Oh dear. You sound like a dangerous driver!
WOMAN I certainly am.

Lesson 36 Grammar and Listening, activity 4

MAN What have you decided to do tomorrow?
WOMAN Well, first I'll get up very early and have a big breakfast. Then, I think I'll go sightseeing.
MAN What do you want to see?
WOMAN Lots of things. I think I'll go to the Louvre first. Then I'll visit Notre Dame Cathedral.
MAN Will you come back to the hotel for lunch?
WOMAN I'm sorry, I won't have time. I'd like to have lunch on a boat on the River Seine.
MAN That sounds great!
WOMAN Then in the afternoon I'll go up the Eiffel Tower to get a view of Paris, visit the Montmartre district, go shopping for souvenirs on the Champs Elysées, have a glass of wine in a cafe and ...
MAN That sounds like a very busy day!

Lesson 37 Sounds

11° -1° 16° 35° -4° 24° -10°

Lesson 37 Reading and Listening, activity 2

MAN I saw a programme about life in the future on television last night. It was very gloomy.
WOMAN Well, I think life in the future will be terrible. There will be too many people in the world and not enough food for everyone.
MAN You're worse than the people on the TV! I think life will be better than today. People will be more healthy. And they'll live longer and happier lives.
WOMAN You're very optimistic. But I think you are wrong. I think life will be very hard for most people.

Lesson 38 Sounds, activity 1

1 Tea is grown in Brazil.
No, it isn't. It's grown in India.
2 The telephone was invented by Marconi.
No, it wasn't. It was invented by Bell.
3 *Guernica* was painted by Monet.
No, it wasn't. It was painted by Picasso.
4 *Hamlet* was written by Spencer.
No, it wasn't. It was written by Shakespeare.
5 Toyota cars are made in the United States.
No, they aren't. They're made in Japan.
6 The Pyramids were built by Alexander the Great. No, they weren't. They were built by the Pharaohs

Lesson 39 Listening and Reading, activity 1

Phone call 1

A Can I speak to Peter, please? This is John Griffiths.
B I'm sorry, he's out at the moment. Can I take a message?
A Yes, please. It's about the concert tonight. I've got the tickets for us. It's at the Palace Hall. It starts at 8.30 so we want to be there for 8.15. There's a train which leaves here at 7.15. I think it's easier than in the car.
B Right. I've got that. Do you want him to ring you back?

A No. I'm out until this evening, so there's no point.
B OK. Goodbye.
A Thank you. Goodbye.

Phone call 2

C Hi, Marjorie! Is Liz there, please? This is Maria.
D I'm sorry, Maria, but she's out just now. Can I help?
C Well,you see, I'm supposed to meet her for lunch tomorrow. The trouble is I've got an appointment at the dentist's at 1.30. But I can meet her earlier for coffee – say 11 o'clock.
D OK. I'll leave her a message.
C So, if she doesn't ring me back, I'll see her at Ascari's at 11. Oh, before I forget. Tell her I've got her books she needs for college. And they aren't expensive, only £5 each.
D Right. Goodbye, Maria.
C Thanks. Bye.

Phone call 3

E Hello. Can I speak to Henry Croft, please? This is Helen Croft speaking.
F Oh, hello, Mrs Croft. I'm afraid your husband is in a meeting at the moment. Would you like to leave a message?
E Yes, please. Can you tell him that I'm at Charles de Gaulle Airport in Paris and my flight is delayed. I don't know what time it will arrive in London. He doesn't need to meet me at Heathrow. I'll get a taxi.
F I've noted that down.
E Oh, by the way. Tell him the new office in Paris is fine and the new manager seems very competent.
F Right. Goodbye Mrs Croft.
E Goodbye.

Phone call 4

G Hello, this is John. Can I speak to Anna, please?
H I'm afraid she's out. Can I give her a message?
G That would be great. Tell her there's an interesting flat for sale in Fulham. It's quite a nice area: not noisy. It's near a tube station and a small shopping centre. There's a park not far away. It isn't very expensive. If she wants to see it, I'm free tomorrow afternoon.
H Right. I've got that. Anything else?
G Umm. I'm at the office this afternoon if she wants to give me a ring.

Answer Key

Lesson 1

VOCABULARY

1 Rome, Italy; Rio de Janeiro, Brazil; Washington, the United States of America; Moscow, Russia; Sydney, Australia; Istanbul, Turkey
2 *Across:* Spain India Argentina Turkey Canada Brazil
Down: Peru Japan Greece France China Italy Russia Korea Britain Mexico Thailand
3 1 Seoul is in Korea. 2 Buenos Aires is in Argentina. 3 Paris is in France. 4 Tokyo is in Japan. 5 Athens is in Greece. 6 Lima is in Peru.

FUNCTIONS

1 1 What is your name? 2 Where are you from? 3 My name is Charlie. 4 I am from Canada. 5 Is your name Maria?
2 1 b 2 c 5 a
4 *Verbs:* is am are be
Subject pronouns: you I

SOUNDS

1 Japan China Canada Korea Germany Russia Brazil Turkey Ukraine Morocco
2

oO	Oo	Ooo	oOo
Japan	China	Canada	Korea
Brazil	Russia	Germany	Morocco
Ukraine	Turkey		

LISTENING

1 A 3 B 1 C 4 D 2
2 *Conversation 1:* France, Spain
Conversation 2: Italy, the United States of America
Conversation 3: Sweden, Canada
Conversation 4: Australia

Lesson 2

VOCABULARY

1 *Jobs:* teacher waiter receptionist doctor chef actor artist police officer nurse journalist
2 1 He's a waiter. 2 She's an artist. 3 He's a chef. 4 She's a doctor. 5 He's a farmer. 6 They're police officers.
3 1 her 2 Moscow 3 we 4 Brazil 5 friend 6 your

GRAMMAR

1 1 They're 2 You're 3 Their 4 your 5 Their
2 1 He's 2 His 3 He's 4 his 5 He's
3 1 She's a secretary. 2 They're from Australia. 3 He's an actor. 4 They're doctors. 5 We're farmers.
4 1 He is 2 They are 3 I am 4 We are 5 They are 6 She is

READING

1 1 Maria is a receptionist.
2 Jim is a jazz musician.
3 Isabella is an economist.
4 Yannick is a journalist.
5 Emma is a nurse.
2 1 No, he is from France.
2 No, she is from Milan.
3 No, she is a nurse.
4 No, he is a jazz musician.
5 No, they are teachers.
3 His name is Yannick. He's from France. He's a journalist for an international magazine. His wife's name is Isabella and she's from Barcelona. She's an economist.

LISTENING

1 I'm from Britain.
I'm a computer technician here at the university.
I'm from Vancouver in Canada.
I'm a student.
France teacher
2 His name's Silvio.
Where's he from?
He's from Italy. What's his job?
He's an accountant.

Lesson 3

VOCABULARY

1 *Nouns:* student children Japan doctor surname phone number brother actor friend address first name job boyfriend
Adjectives: married single good-looking

GRAMMAR

1 1 c 2 d 3 e 4 a 5 f 6 b
2 1 Where 2 How 3 What 4 Who 5 Where 6 What
4 *Suggested answers*
1 Is she married? 2 Are you single? 3 Are his children students? 4 Is he from Oxford? 5 Are you an economist? 6 Is she a teacher?
5 1 No, she isn't. She's from Romania. 2 No, he isn't. He's a nurse. 3 No, they aren't. They're Argentinian. 4 No, she isn't. She's seventeen. 5 No, he isn't. He's married.

LISTENING

1 at a job interview
2 What's your name? What's your job? How old are you? Are you married? Are you British?
3 1 No, she isn't. She's single.
2 No, she isn't. She's 25.
3 No, she isn't. She's Italian.

WRITING

1 Picture A: Janvi Singh
Picture C: May Downs
Picture D: Michael Haines

Lesson 4

VOCABULARY

1 1 room 2 chair 3 interesting 4 that
3 1 kind/good 2 good/kind 3 interesting 4 comfortable 5 beautiful

GRAMMAR AND SOUNDS

1 43 13 97 56 51 12 63 17 8 94 77 15 85 3 39
2 classrooms teachers addresses numbers colleges classes chairs
3 1 There is 2 There are 3 There is 4 There are 5 There is
4 /θ/: thirteen three thanks think /ð/: this their with there the they

READING

1 It is a bilingual school.
2 new bilingual old modern big friendly good big comfortable special small expensive
3 1 No, it isn't. 2 It's for children. 3 They are six and nine years old. 4 It's in the town centre. 5 It's an old building but inside it's modern.

Lesson 5

VOCABULARY

1 *Electronic products:* calculator camera computer mobile phone personal stereo radio
Office things: calculator computer diary notebook pen pencil
Jobs: accountant doctor farmer vet
Places: city country library school
2 A keys B diary C comb D calculator E glasses F credit card G gloves H brush I watch J camera
3 A near B in C under D on
4 1 How 2 What 3 What 4 Where

GRAMMAR

1 1 He has got 2 They have got 3 She is 4 I have got 5 She has got 6 He is

SOUNDS

1 1 wallet 2 colour 3 comb 4 camera 5 watch 6 diary

LISTENING

glasses colour blue green bag on under

Lesson 6

VOCABULARY

1

Male	**Female**
man	woman
boy	girl
father	mother
brother	sister
nephew	niece
son	daughter
husband	wife
uncle	aunt
grandfather	grandmother
cousin	cousin

2 1 aunt 2 niece 3 grandmother 4 son 5 brother 6 cousin
3 men women children families people wives countries

READING AND GRAMMAR

2 *Family A:* Jenny is thirty-two years old and has got a job in a post office in a small village. She's divorced and has got an eight-year-old daughter, Cilla, and a three-year-old son, Jamie. She's got a small house with a big garden in the village. She's got a lot of friends in the village. Jenny's mother, Kate, lives in the same village. She helps Jenny with the children when she's at work.
3 1 Jenny is divorced. (Elizabeth's husband is Peter.) 2 Elizabeth has a part-time job in a school. (Peter is an architect.) 3 Peter has got four children. (Jenny has got two children.) 4 Jenny has got a job in a post office. (Elizabeth has got a part-time job in a school.) 5 Jenny has got a house in a village. (Peter and Elizabeth have got a house near London.)
4 1 Elizabeth is Peter's wife.
2 Fiona and Michael are Peter's parents.
3 Cilla is Jenny's daughter/Kate's granddaughter/Jamie's sister.
4 Jamie is Jenny's son/Kate's grandson/Cilla's brother.

LISTENING

1 Speaker 1: Helen
Speaker 2: Greg
2 1 teacher 2 two 3 American 4 computer 6 married

Lesson 7

VOCABULARY

1 1 It's twenty past four in the afternoon.
2 It's a quarter to eleven in the morning.
3 It's nine o'clock in the evening.
4 It's half past eleven in the morning.
5 It's a quarter past six in the morning.
2 1 get up 2 have breakfast 3 start work 4 have lunch 5 finish work 6 have dinner 7 go to bed

READING

1 *Prepositions of time:* at nine in the morning; at five in the evening; at eight; at five; at weekends; on Saturday mornings; on Wednesday afternoons; at lunchtime; at midday; In the evening; at about eight o'clock

GRAMMAR

1 1 in 2 at 3 at 4 at 5 in 6 on 7 at 8 on

SOUNDS

1 1 Do you work at the weekend?
2 Do people work on Sunday mornings?
3 Do they have lunch at home?
4 Do we finish work at five today?
5 Do you have a siesta in the afternoon?
2 1 work 2 clock 3 girl 4 breakfast
3 1 3.30 2 10.15 3 7.45 4 2.10 5 9.55 6 1.35 7 11.30 8 7.00 9 4.05 10 6.40

Lesson 8

GRAMMAR

1 1 are 2 is 3 are 4 aren't 5 Are 6 isn't 7 Is 8 is
2 1 any 2 some 3 some 4 any 5 any 6 some

LISTENING

1 *Speaker 1:* study
Speaker 2: sitting room
Speaker 3: bedroom
2 *Room 1:* 1 study 2 upstairs, bathroom 3 bookcases 4 window, computer 5 mirror, armchair
Room 2: 1 sitting room 2 window, garden 3 sofa, fire 4 curtains, piano 5 television, video
Room 3: 1 bedroom 2 upstairs 3 bed, lamp 4 cupboard 5 plants

SOUNDS

1 /ɑː/: armchair bath carpet garden large plant
/eɪ/: bookcase game plane radio table washbasin

WRITING AND READING

2 Italy
3 1 F 2 T 3 F 4 F 5 T

Lesson 9

LISTENING

1 *Across:* relax live watch get drink make play do go eat sing
Down: read learn wash work have see come like start finish
2 1 have 2 watch 3 make 4 eat, drink 5 play 6 learn

GRAMMAR

1 1 He/She has a sauna on Wednesday evenings. 2 He/She watches sport on television on Saturday afternoons. 3 He/She makes the Sunday lunch for the family. 4 He/She eats a sandwich and drinks mineral water for lunch. 5 He/She plays the guitar in a rock band with friends. 6 He/She learns Spanish at evening classes.
2 1 Where 2 How 3 Who 4 What 5 When

READING

1 a man
2 He makes dinner. He watches the sport on television. He goes running. He reads. He watches television.
3 She goes to language classes. She goes to a friend's house for dinner. She works on her computer.
4 They have a drink. They sit and have dinner in front of the television. They go to the cinema. They have a drink in a bar. They get up at midday. They go to the supermarket. They go to a restaurant or to a nightclub. They go to her parents' house.

LISTENING

1 *Woman 1:* has a cup of tea; makes dinner; goes to a friend's house; goes running; goes to a jazz club
Woman 2: reads the newspaper; has a language class; has dinner with a friend; works on her computer
2 Woman 2

SOUNDS

1 1 gets 2 has 3 makes 4 speaks

Lesson 10

SOUNDS

1 *Two syllables:* football country singer tennis programme skating
Three syllables: computer magazine unemployed afternoon cinema classical

READING

1 c 2 d 3 e 4 a 5 b

GRAMMAR

1

Subject	**Object**
I	me
you	you
he	him
she	her
it	it
we	us
they	them

2 1 it 2 them 3 it 4 her 5 them 6 him
3 1 Do you like classical music?
2 What type of music do you like?
3 I do not like skiing at all.
4 Do you like going to the cinema?
5 I do not like it very much.
4 1 I like eating Chinese food.
2 I like watching television.
3 I like going to the cinema.
4 I like playing computer games.
5 I like drinking tea.

LISTENING

1 1a 2b
2 *Man:* modern art, classical art, classical music
Woman: classical art, reggae, dancing

Lesson 11

VOCABULARY AND GRAMMAR

1 late punctual early on time

SOUNDS

2 *Happy:* Sentences 1 and 3
Unhappy: Sentences 2, 4, 5 and 6

LISTENING

1 *Suggested answers*
taxi driver: car city streets map nightwork drive
teacher: classroom pupils school desk folder teach
chef: food restaurant dinner cook lunch
musician: dancing club guitar rock concert play
2 *Suggested answers*
a teacher b musician c chef d taxi driver

3 *Speaker 1:* musician
Speaker 2: chef
4 *Musician:* Sentences 1, 4, 6 and 7
Chef: Sentences 2, 5, 8 and 10
5 teacher
6 1 get up 2 have 3 leaves
4 read 5 leave 6 have
7 works 8 get 9 go 10 get

Lesson 12

READING

1 Picture A
2 many journeys take a day; there is a bus only once or twice a week; dangerous; break down; very slow and uncomfortable; very crowded
3 It is cheap.

GRAMMAR

1 1 a bus – buses
2 a coach – coaches
3 a ferry – ferries
4 an airport – airports
5 a house – houses
6 an office – offices
7 a delay – delays
8 an hour – hours
2 1 the, the 2 - 3 a 4 - 5 a
6 the 7 a, a 8 The 9 - 10 the, -
3 *Suggested answers*
1 How long does it take?
2 How do you get to work?
3 Do you go very often?
4 How much is it?
5 How far is it?

SOUNDS

1 1 It's about eighty miles.
2 The office is near the station.
3 It's the age of the train.
4 It's quite expensive.
2 slow coach train plane
bus month drive ride
stop long quick live

Lesson 13

VOCABULARY AND GRAMMAR

1 *Across:* 3 swim 6 cook 8 drink
9 be 12 do 13 ride 17 read
18 win 19 fly
Down: 1 ski 2 hold 4 walk
5 meet 7 knit 10 go 11 drive
14 draw 15 eat 16 play 17 run
2 1 can't 2 can 3 can, can't 4 can
5 can, can't

SOUNDS

1 cupboard daylight foreign hour knit listen night often walk write
2 1 ✗ 2 ✓ 3 ✗ 4 ✗ 5 ✗ 6 ✓

READING AND WRITING

1 A camera B bed C television
D dishwasher E mirror F fire
2 1 dishwasher 2 bed 3 television
4 camera 5 fire 6 mirror
3 is wash sleep lie put on watch use take carry sit look see
4 1 It is usually in the kitchen.
2 It is often upstairs in a house.
3 This is often in the sitting room.
4 ...you can carry it in your bag.
5 It is often in the sitting room.
6 It can be on a wall in any room in the house. There is always one in the bathroom.

Lesson 14

VOCABULARY

1 send eat buy take out change
2 *Post office:* stamps send buy letters envelopes
Newsagent's: buy magazine newspaper sweets
Chemist's: sun cream medicine buy aspirin
Bank: account money traveller's cheques take out change
Station: buy platform ticket train
Restaurant: meal menu buy dinner

GRAMMAR AND READING

2 in the west; at the end; in; in; behind; opposite; opposite; on; between; Behind; in; opposite; At the end; Before; on the corner; opposite; out of
3 1 museum 2 chemist's 3 tourist information centre 4 post office
5 indoor market 6 shopping mall 7 park 8 hotel 9 bank
4 1 opposite 2 between
3 opposite 4 on the corner of
5 behind 6 next to, opposite

LISTENING

1 1 stamps, the post office
2 aspirin, a chemist's
3 an Italian restaurant
2 *Conversation 1:* 1 along 2 right, straight ahead 3 opposite, behind
Conversation 2: 1 along
2 opposite 3 on the left
3 husband French restaurant twenty minutes' ten metres next to Italian

Lesson 15

GRAMMAR

1 enjoying staying passing having living learning shopping sitting flying travelling taking lying writing
2 1 are staying 2 is lying
3 are having 4 are flying
5 are enjoying

SOUNDS

1 *Two syllables:* ugly lively modern mountains boring
Three syllables: beautiful attractive wonderful
Four syllables: industrial
2 1 We're having a wonderful time.
2 I'm not enjoying the flight.
3 She's learning to swim.
4 They're staying at an expensive hotel.
5 He's travelling for his job.
6 I'm writing this on the beach.

VOCABULARY

beautiful – ugly; east – west; interesting – boring; old-fashioned – modern; north– south; cold – hot; dark – light; quiet – noisy

LISTENING

1 *Picture A:* sea coast port
Picture B: chalet skiing mountains snow cold holiday
Picture C: modern industrial town river
2 *Suggested answers*
Picture A: lively interesting
Picture B: beautiful
Picture C: ugly
3 *Conversation 1:* city sea-port
Conversation 2: mountain ski resort
4 *Conversation 1:* 1 false (her mother) 2 false (in the centre)
3 true 4 true
Conversation 2: 1 false (her husband) 2 true 3 true
4 false (her mother is sleeping, her father is having a drink)

READING AND WRITING

1 It is on the Mediterranean coast in the south-east of France near Italy. It is between the mountains and the sea.
2 beautiful location pleasant climate gambling casinos motor race no taxes

Lesson 16

VOCABULARY AND READING

1 1 d 2 a 3 c 4 b
2 *dog:* noisy naughty not obedient
girlfriend: shy attractive
girlfriend's hair: dark
weather on caravan holiday: horrid
holiday in Greece: exciting wonderful
children: not well-behaved
parents: bad-tempered
caravan holiday: terrible
weather in Greece: hot

GRAMMAR

1 1 was 2 were 3 was
4 were 5 were 6 was
2 1 Where were you born?
2 What were you like at school?
3 Who was your best friend at school?
4 What were you good at?
5 Were you often in trouble in school?

VOCABULARY AND SOUNDS

1 stubborn obedient
lazy cheerful horrid
untidy polite naughty
disappointing

LISTENING

1 1 b 2 a 3 f 4 c 5 e 6 d

Lesson 17

VOCABULARY

1 1 rice 2 bacon 3 potato
4 oil 5 salt 6 onion

READING AND WRITING

1 1 true 2 false 3 false
4 false 5 true 6 true
7 true 8 false
2 *common:* chopsticks with the Chinese population; smoking
crowded, noisy and hot: restaurants in the early evening
relaxed: restaurants
3 *C:* table meal spoon fingers restaurants
U: food salt fish sauce alcohol drink
4 2 Only the Chinese population use chopsticks.
3 They use their fingers.
4 They can drink alcohol.
8 Restaurants are very informal.

GRAMMAR AND LISTENING

1 *U:* wine oil yoghurt
butter pork milk
water beef bread
tea salt rice
soup pasta cheese
C: apple egg onion
lemon carrot steak
2 1 some 2 some 3 a
4 any 5 some 6 a
3 at a restaurant
4 1 some 2 any 3 some
4 a 5 any 6 a
7 any 8 some 9 any
10 some 11 an 12 any

Lesson 18

VOCABULARY

1 1 hit 2 teenager 3 album
4 musician 5 group 6 award
7 guitar
2 1 g 2 d 3 a 4 f
5 c 6 h 7 e 8 b

GRAMMAR AND READING

1 appeared created died learned lived composed married moved played started worked finished
2 1 married 2 appeared/played
3 learned 4 worked 5 started
6 created
3 1 learned 2 started
3 appeared/played 4 lived
5 moved 6 moved 7 married
8 worked 9 composed 10 died

SOUNDS

1 1 talked 2 appeared 3 visited
4 watched
2 1 She was born in London.
2 He learned to play the piano.
3 She received an award.
4 They created the group *The Police*.
5 He started work as a teacher.

LISTENING

2 1 Kevin Costner 2 Jodie Foster
3 1 was born 2 studied
3 received 4 appeared
5 appeared

Lesson 19

VOCABULARY

2 *Suggested answers*
Picture A: slim curly glasses

Picture B: middle-aged
well-built dark
Picture C: elderly fair curly
not very tall
3 *Suggested answers*
Picture A: The woman isn't slim. She has straight hair. She doesn't have glasses
Picture B: The man is young and slim. He has fair hair.
Picture C: The woman is young/middle-aged. She has dark straight hair. She is tall.

FUNCTIONS
1 *Suggested answers*
1 What's he like?
2 What does she look like?
3 How tall is she?
4 How old is he?
5 Who does she look like?
6 How does she dress?

SOUNDS
/ɪ/: built slim thin sixty
/aɪ/: kind time nice
smile polite child

LISTENING
1 1 a lost child 2 an old classmate
3 a criminal
2 1 two 2 short, dark 3 blue, yellow, white
3 2 3 6

Lesson 20

VOCABULARY
1 *Across:* did made bought took said lost went spent became
Down: found had gave got came wrote
2 1 wrote 2 did/bought 3 went
4 took/got 5 made 6 lost
3 1 b 2 e 3 f 4 a 5 c 6 d

GRAMMAR
1 1 Did you visit a museum yesterday?
2 Did you write some postcards at the weekend?
3 Did you do some shopping yesterday?
4 Did you go to a restaurant on Saturday?
5 Did you take a train last week?

READING
1 1 Diana. 2 She is writing to Robert. 3 No, she is travelling with Mike.
2 1 It was sunny and warm.
2 She spent four days in London.
3 She took the Eurostar to Paris.
4 She stayed with her cousin.
5 She lost her passport in the Metro.
6 She went to Barcelona after Paris.
7 She stayed in a hotel.
8 She spent two days by the sea.

SOUNDS
1 good 2 close 3 born
4 give 5 have

Lesson 21

GRAMMAR AND VOCABULARY
1 encouraged informed thought sold married left found refused
2 1 c 2 d 3 e 4 g 5 b 6 a 7 f

SOUNDS
1 and 2 *Two syllables:* divorced explain famous final happen inform notice refuse
Three syllables: continue disappear encourage successful

READING
1 William Shakespeare
was was went married had left went did lived worked stopped was wrote wrote finished left went died
2 2 When was he born?
3 Where did he go to school?
4 Who did he marry?
5 Where did he work as an actor?
6 When did he stop acting?
7 Why did he stop acting?
8 When did he write his first play?
9 Where did he go in 1612?
10 When did he die?
3 Between 1585 and 1590.
4 1 He was born in Stratford.
2 He was born in 1564.
3 He went to the local grammar school.
4 He married Anne Hathaway.
5 He worked in London.
6 He stopped acting in 1603.
7 Because he was famous for his writing.
8 He wrote his first play in 1590–91.
9 He went back to Stratford.
10 He died in 1616.

WRITING
1 was went was lived went wrote was received
2 *Suggested answer*
Mark Twain was born in Missouri, USA in 1835. We know that he worked as a ship's pilot on the Mississippi in 1857 and he became a journalist in 1862. He went on a tour of Europe in 1865 and in 1876 he wrote The Adventures of Tom Sawyer. He died in 1910.

Lesson 22

VOCABULARY AND SOUNDS
1 fifth sixth eighth ninth twelfth thirteenth fifteenth
2 *Nouns:* discovery, discoverer explosion invention, inventor landing painting, painter take-off win, winner, winnings
3 1 won 2 discovered
3 exploded 4 painted
5 invented 6 landed

READING
1 B
2 *Columbia*, the first space shuttle took off.
Challenger exploded at take-off.
NASA put the Hubble Space Telescope into space.
Endeavor replaced *Challenger*.

GRAMMAR
1 in June, in 1995, in the evening, in the morning
on Friday, on the 26th March
at the weekend, at night
yesterday
night/evening/morning
last month/weekend/night
a month/week ago 10 years ago

LISTENING
1 1 yesterday 2 about ten years ago 3 1985 4 1988 5 Last year
6 two months 7 in the spring

Lesson 23

VOCABULARY
1 *Across:* 1 jacket 6 T-shirt
8 shoe 9 skirt 11 blouse
Down: 1 jeans 2 coat
3 trousers 4 shorts 5 suit
7 boots 8 sock 10 tie

LISTENING
1, 2 and 3 Model 1 (C): red skirt, pink sweater, purple sunglasses
Model 2 (B): grey trousers, yellow jacket, grey and yellow blouse
Model 3 (D): blue dress, brown shoes, pink scarf
Model 4 (A): black jeans, orange socks, black trainers, green T-shirt

READING AND GRAMMAR
1 1 Pat is writing to Sarah.
2 Pat is on holiday in New Zealand.
3 She is Pat's mother's cousin.
2 *Present continuous:* I'm having
I'm staying she's having
I'm staying I'm staying
I'm flying
Present simple: she's
Aunt Grace is She's got
she wears she smiles she talks
she is she reads
she doesn't know
she never goes she says it's
she's we visit the scenery is
3 expensive – the trip to Britain
wonderful – her holiday
beautiful – the scenery
lovely – Aunt Grace's eyes
interesting – Aunt Grace
happy – Aunt Grace
4 1 are staying 2 live 3 wears
4 is looking 5 goes 6 is laughing

Lesson 24

VOCABULARY
1 1 study 2 stop 3 worry
4 save 5 spend 6 invite
2 1 d 2 f 3 e 4 b 5 a 6 c

GRAMMAR
1 *Suggested answers*
1 He's going to fly to Hawaii.
2 They're going to see a football match.
3 They're going to play tennis.
4 She's going to do the shopping.

SOUNDS
1 *Tick:* 2 4 *Cross:* 1 3 5

LISTENING
1 c
2 1 65 2 work 3 trip/holiday
4 Central and South America
5 move, London 6 flat, park

WRITING
1 magazine fashion writer
2 *Suggested answers*
On Monday she's going to visit the hat exhibition at the new art and design college at 2 pm.
On Tuesday at 7.15 am she's going to take the Eurostar to Paris. At 11 am she's going to do an interview with a Paris clothes designer.
On Wednesday she's going to an editorial meeting for the January edition of the magazine.
On Thursday she's going to the Piccadilly clothes show.
On Friday she's going to finish her article on hats.
On Saturday she's going to Pete and Jenny's party.
On Sunday she's going to visit her parents in Oxford.

Lesson 25

VOCABULARY
1 a waiter b bill c service, tip
d starter e coffee f reservation
g menu h course, dessert
i taste j order
2 1 f 2 a 3 g 4 j 5 i 6 d
7 h 8 e 9 b 10 c

READING AND LISTENING
1 1 in a pub 2 at home
2 and 3 *Dialogue 1:* in the corner (over there) three (two)
gin and tonic (gin and orange)
Yes, please (No, thank you)
a mineral water (a Coke)
some crisps (a sandwich)
Dialogue 2: salad (potatoes)
chips (beans) fridge (cupboard)
glass of water (a beer)
I'm afraid there isn't any left
(Yes. It's in the fridge.)

FUNCTIONS
1 *Waiter:* 1 3 4 6
Customer: 2 5 7 8
2 *Suggested answers*
2 Certainly, madam.
3 I'd like salad, please.
4 Can I have a beer, please?
5 Certainly, sir.
6 Chocolate, please.
7 What flavour would you like?
8 Yes, sir.
3 *Suggested answers*
1 Would you like a dessert?
2 Can I have some chips, please?
3 What flavour would you like?
4 Can I help you?
5 Can you bring me the wine list, please?
6 Do you like the salad?

Lesson 26

GRAMMAR

1 yourself himself herself itself ourselves yourselves themselves
2 1 myself 2 themselves 3 himself 4 yourself 5 ourselves
3 *Suggested answers*
1 They enjoyed themselves at the party. 2 She is teaching herself to speak French. 3 He talks to himself.

VOCABULARY

1 newspaper toothpaste sunglasses handbag raincoat hamburger
3 a bottle of shampoo a packet of biscuits a box of matches a tube of toothpaste a bar of chocolate a can of tomatoes

SOUNDS

1 The first word is stressed.
2 1 too 2 like 3 suit 4 fit 5 colour

LISTENING AND FUNCTIONS

1 in a shop
2 and 3 1 False (He wants to buy a winter coat.) 2 True 3 True 4 False (It's too big.) 5 True 6 True 7 False (He doesn't buy it because it's expensive.)
4 1 I'll take it. 2 I think I'll leave it.

Lesson 27

VOCABULARY

1 *binoculars:* metal, plastic and glass
wallet: leather or plastic
umbrella: nylon and metal
book: paper
2 *Across:* 1 binoculars 3 umbrella 5 Property 8 wood 10 his 11 metal
Down: 1 box 2 camera 4 new 6 purse 7 thick 9 out

SOUNDS

2 1 your, his 2 your, hers 3 her, mine 4 their, ours 5 your, yours 6 our, theirs

GRAMMAR

1 *Suggested answers*
1 What shape is it?
2 What colour is it?
3 What's it made of?
4 Is this yours?
5 Whose books are they?
6 What's in your bag?
2 2 It's his. 3 It's theirs. 4 They're ours. 5 They're hers. 6 It's yours.

READING AND WRITING

1 3
2 A stamps, purse B umbrellas C papers, keys, phone card, cash card, bag, car keys D nothing
D is the most careful.

Lesson 28

VOCABULARY

2 1 c 2 d 3 e 4 a 5 b
3 *Suggested answers*
1 I've got a sore throat.
2 My back hurts.
3 I feel faint.
4 I feel dizzy.
5 I've got a cough.

GRAMMAR AND FUNCTIONS

3 1 d 2 a 3 c 4 b

SOUNDS

2 *Two syllables:* aspirin medicine complaint private treatment
Three syllables: accident exercise hospital temperature

READING AND WRITING

1 A sun B insects
3 You shouldn't stay in the sun too long
you should stay out of the sun at midday
you should lie down in a cool place
you should call a doctor
you should take medicine every day

Lesson 29

VOCABULARY AND SOUNDS

1 *Across:* long, good light dry big high slow hot fast easy small modern
Down: heavy bad low wet old dirty safe dark young cold
2 good – better – best
bad – worse – worst
heavy – heavier – heaviest
old – older – oldest
low – lower – lowest
easy – easier – easiest
big – bigger – biggest
wet – wetter – wettest
3 2 metre 3 millimetre 4 kilometres per hour 5 kilometre 6 square kilometre 7 kilogram 8 litre
4 1 25°C 2 1,343 m 3 600 mm 4 242,429 sq km 5 130 kph 6 920 km 7 1 kg

READING AND GRAMMAR

1 1 C 2 A 3 E 4 D 5 B
2 The world's second longest river
the world's widest river
it covers the largest area
the country with the highest population
the 6th highest in the world
South America's biggest city
more densely populated
The warmest months
3 *Suggested answers*
1 Brazil is smaller than Canada.
2 Brazil has a bigger population than Chile.
3 The Nile is narrower than the Amazon.
4 Rio is smaller than São Paulo.
5 Most Brazilians live in the cities or on the coast.
4 *Suggested answers*
1 Brazil is bigger than Argentina.
2 The Amazon is wider than the Nile.
3 Brazil has got a bigger population than Peru.
4 Rio is smaller than São Paulo.
5 June is colder than December.
5 1 Rio is not as big as São Paulo.
2 São Paulo is not as warm as Rio.
3 The climate in the Amazon basin is not as dry as the climate on the coast.
4 The Amazon is not as long as the Nile.
5 It is not as warm in June as it is in December.

Lesson 30

VOCABULARY

1 hang gliding motor racing windsurfing horse riding basketball

GRAMMAR

1 1 most 2 more 3 most 4 most 5 more 6 more

READING AND WRITING

1 2
2 more beautiful more civilised
more good-looking
more sophisticated
more mouthwatering
more exotic more exciting
more interesting
more expressive
more monumental
more spectacular
3 *Suggested answers*
Shops are more exciting.
The ringing of telephones is stranger.
Bread is tastier.
Shop assistants are more efficient.
Bank clerks are friendlier.
Children are politer.
Street signs are stranger.

Lesson 31

GRAMMAR

2 1 h 2 d 3 f 4 g 5 b 6 c 7 a 8 e
3 1 mustn't 2 mustn't 3 must 4 mustn't 5 mustn't 6 must 7 must 8 mustn't
4 rules

READING

1 A 1 B 4
2 *Suggested answers*
B: keep your dog on a lead
C: no golf.
D: no cycling.
E: put litter in bins
F: You are not allowed to sleep overnight on the benches.
3 You must wear proper swimsuits. An adult must stay with children under six at all times.
4 *Suggested answers*
Notice A
You must put litter in the bins.
You mustn't play golf.
You mustn't cycle.
You must keep your dog on a lead.
You mustn't sleep overnight on the benches.
You mustn't stay inside after closing time.
You mustn't walk on the flower beds.
You mustn't climb the trees.
Notice B
You mustn't wear shorts.
You mustn't run or jump.
You mustn't smoke in the pool area.
You mustn't eat or drink near the pool.

Lesson 32

READING

1 a waitress, an actress, a nanny, a ticket seller, a cook, a zoo-keeper, in telesales
2 Jane Brooks has had fifty-four jobs. still hasn't found her ideal career. She has been a model ... I just haven't found ...
3 The shortest she had was as a cook in a canteen. She left it after just two hours.
The longest job she had was as a zoo-keeper. She stayed in that job for two months.

GRAMMAR

1 *Past participle:* been drunk had driven read left flown taken bought made written sold fought met found eaten gone seen worn
Past simple: ate had read left saw wore bought made went sold fought met found took flew drove wrote
2 1 Have you ever been to a foreign country?
2 He has never appeared on television.
3 I have visited a lot of countries.
4 They went to Spain last year.
5 When did they go to Spain?
3 1 drunk 2 driven 3 met/seen 4 worn/made 5 flown/been 6 eaten/had 7 written 8 taken
4 1 have never been 2 went 3 has found 4 met 5 has never flown 6 drank
5 1 been, went 2 gone, gone, went

LISTENING

2 *Man:* Switzerland
Woman: Russia and Australia
3 kangaroos, mountain scenery, Moscow, surfing beaches, Red Square, a ski resort

Lesson 33

SOUNDS

3 /eɪ/: age face pay plate stay take
/æ/: back bag crash exam
/ɑː/: park car sharp

GRAMMAR AND VOCABULARY

1 stolen fallen left come kept broken run caught hurt paid lost found

2 1 has stolen 2 has caught
3 have lost 4 has fallen
5 have found
6 have broken
3 a ✓ have never visited
b ✗ visited c ✓ have read d ✓ have just had
e ✓ Have you done ... yet
f ✓ has hurt g ✗ did you go
h ✗ visited, had
4 1 went 2 have lost 3 has ever visited 4 did you come back
5 Have you taken 6 went, took
7 have just booked

READING AND LISTENING
1 1d 2b 3a 4c
3 *Suggested answers*
1 Pete has had an awful day.
2 Jan has been at the office all day.
3 Pete is tired because he has done the housework.
4 Jan has just arrived home from work.
5 Pete hasn't had time to take the car to the garage or to do the shopping.
6 Pete hasn't made the evening meal.

Lesson 34

VOCABULARY
1 *Across:* 2 matches 4 knife 6 ice
7 rubbish 9 glass
Down: 1 blanket 3 rain 5 fork
8 bag
2 1 Be careful! 2 Slow down!
3 Please sit down. 4 Excuse me.
5 Don't worry! 6 Be quiet!

GRAMMAR
1 1c 2e 3a 4f 5d 6b

LISTENING
1 1 Kenya 2 the airport
3 the supermarket 4 the station
2 1 They're going to Kenya to see the wildlife.
2 She's going to the airport to meet her sister.
3 He's going to the supermarket to buy some food.
4 She's going to the station to get the tickets.

READING AND WRITING
1 no
3 1E 2B 3D 4A 5C

Lesson 35

VOCABULARY AND GRAMMAR
1 good – bad quiet – noisy
careful – careless polite – rude
fast – slow early – late
2 good – well bad – badly
happy – happily fast – fast
easy – easily early – early
angry – angrily late – late
careless – carelessly
fluent – fluently clear – clearly
patient – patiently
3 1 fluently 2 good, bad
3 patiently/clearly 4 happy
5 easy, clearly 6 late/early

LISTENING
1 swimming, dancing, cooking, driving
2 1 well, fast 2 good 3 badly
4 fast, slowly 5 dangerous

READING
1 southern Italy
2 quickly purposefully
passionately seriously
slowly carefully noisily
3 *Suggested answers*
They walk quickly and purposefully.
They take life seriously.
They have meetings.
They do business.
They talk on car phones.
They drive slowly.
They park carefully.
4 *Suggested answers*
They sit for hours in cafés.
They drink espressos and eat mountains of pasta.
They argue passionately.
They hang washing in the streets. They shout noisily.
They honk the horns of their scooters.

Lesson 36

VOCABULARY AND READING
1 passport control first class
check-in departure lounge
petrol station baggage reclaim
ticket office arrival hall
boarding pass
2 c h e i f a g d b
3 *Train:* 2 3 8 *Plane:* 1 4
Car: 5 7 9 *Boat:* 6 10
4 *Positive:* 3 6 8
Negative: 1 2 4 10

SOUNDS
1a 2a 3b 4a 5b

GRAMMAR AND LISTENING
1 1 When will he go sightseeing?
2 Will you have a single room?
3 How long will you stay in London?
4 How will you get from the airport/hotel to the hotel/airport?
5 Where will you have dinner this evening.
2 1d 2e 3a 4b 5c
4 b
5 1 She'll get up very early.
2 She'll have a big breakfast.
3 She'll visit the Louvre in the morning.
4 She'll have lunch on a boat on the River Seine.
5 She'll go up the Eiffel Tower in the afternoon.

Lesson 37

VOCABULARY
1 sunny cloudy rainy foggy
cold hot windy warm
snowy wet
2 1D 2C 3F 4A 5B 6E
3 *Suggested answers*
a picnic: sunshine, warm, not too hot
sailing: sunny and windy, warm
seaside holiday: sunny and hot
growing tomatoes: rain and sun
working indoors: rain, cold

SOUNDS
1 11° -1° 16° 35° -4° 24° -10°

GRAMMAR
1 1 There will be sunshine. It will be cold and very windy.
2 It will be sunny and warm. It will be a nice day.
3 There will be snow. It will be very cold.
4 It will be rainy and warm.
2 *Suggested answers*
1 It won't rain. It won't be hot.
2 It won't be cold.
3 There won't be any sunshine. It won't be a nice day.
4 It won't be sunny but it won't be cold.
4 *Suggested answers*
1 will get 2 will disappear
3 will become 4 will grow
5 will increase 6 will melt

READING AND LISTENING
1 *Suggested answers*
Pessimistic: 1 3 6 7 8 10
Optimistic: 2 4 5 9
2 The man is optimistic, the woman is pessimistic.
3 *Woman:* 1 3 *Man:* 2 9

Lesson 38

SOUNDS
1 2 No, it wasn't. It was invented by Bell.
3 No, it wasn't. It was painted by Picasso.
4 No, it wasn't. It was written by Shakespeare.
5 No, they aren't. They are made in Japan.
6 No, they weren't. They were built by the Pharaohs.
2 pottery computer tobacco
coffee compose invent
discover Japanese consume
appreciate introduce

VOCABULARY AND GRAMMAR
2 1 grow 2 built 3 discovered
4 grow 5 discovered 6 invented
3 *Present:* 1, 4 *Past:* 2, 3, 5, 6
4 2 The Blue Mosque in Istanbul was built by Sultan Ahmed.
3 Penicillin was discovered by Fleming in 1928.
4 Oranges are grown in the region of Valencia in Spain.
5 Australia was discovered by the Europeans in the 17th century.
6 Gunpowder was invented by the Chinese in the 9th century.

READING AND WRITING
1 drunk introduced appreciated
grown sold dried enjoyed
consumed heated
2 is grown are dried and heated
was first grown was introduced
is grown is sold
3 B: coffee C: tobacco

Lesson 39

GRAMMAR
1 1 'It's open all year.'
2 'It starts at half past nine.'
3 'Dinner is served at seven.'
4 'We're late because of the traffic.'
5 'I don't like the food.'
6 'I'm not staying another night.'
2 1 was 2 leaves 3 cost 4 were
5 was 6 is 7 was 8 finished
3 1 He said it wasn't far from the town centre.
2 She said she didn't like opera.
3 She said the bus arrived at 9 o'clock.
4 The manager said that they had a double room.
5 He said it cost thirty pounds a night.
6 She said the train took half an hour.
7 They said they didn't want a television in the room.
8 He said they were early and that it didn't leave until six thirty.

LISTENING AND READING
1 1c 2d 3b 4a
3 and 4 8.00 (8.30); cheaper (easier); 7.00 (7.15); in the office all day (out all day)
5 Maria phoned... She said she could meet you for coffee...
She said that if you didn't phone back... She also said she had got the books... And they only cost £5 each

Lesson 40

READING
1 1 Maria. 2 She is writing to Anna.
3 She is in Hastings in Britain.
4 She is on an English course.
2 1d 2b 3c 4a
3 *Suggested answers*
Present simple: As you know, we work, we go, the course finishes, I don't know
Present continuous: I'm enjoying, I'm staying
Present perfect: I haven't written, I have been busy, I've met, I've seen
Past simple: I left home, I travelled, the ferry journey wasn't nice, I saw
Future: I won't travel, what I'll do, I'll stay, It'll be, My English will be

GRAMMAR
1 1 went: past simple
2 'm staying: present continuous
3 'll come: future

4 haven't met: present perfect
5 like: present simple

2 1 b 2 e 3 a 4 c 5 d

3 won bought said stepped sold sent told got made arrived left lost read climbed hurt found

4 1 met 2 has just come back 3 have lost 4 won 5 Have you read 6 arrived 7 haven't done 8 did they leave

5 1 am staying 2 takes 3 don't like 4 is not playing 5 work 6 Do you often go

6 1 3 6

Macmillan Education
Between Towns Road, Oxford OX4 3PP
A division of Macmillan Publishers Limited
Companies and representatives throughout the world

ISBN 3 19 012501 5

First published 1997

German translations by Fiona Jureczek, Wolnzach

Designed by Giles Davies

Cover design by Stafford & Stafford

Illustrations by
Phil Bannister, pp12, 13, 38, 46
Kathy Baxendale, pp28, 49, 74
Jerry Collins, pp26, 46, 54, 68
Frances Lloyd, pp7, 53, 56, 63
Judy Stevens, pp10, 27
Darrel Warner, pp3, 4, 48
Gary Wing, p11

Acknowledgements

The authors and publishers would like to thank the following for their kind permission to reproduce material in this book:

David Higham Associates on behalf of Keith Waterhouse for an adapted extract from *The Theory and Practice of Travel* published by Coronet Books; Reed Consumer Books Ltd. for an adapted extract from *Neither Here Nor There* by Bill Bryson published by Martin Secker & Warburg Ltd.

Photographs by: Image Bank: p44(l); Kobal Collection: pp37(tl,bc); Sarah Meadows: p20; Rex Features: p37(tr); Tony Stone: pp14, 24(c), 31(a,c), 41, 44(r), 60; Zefa: pp24(a,b), 31(b), 35,

While every effort has been made to trace the owners of copyright material in this book, there have been some cases when the publishers have been unable to contact the owners. We should be grateful to hear from anyone who recognises their copyright material and who is unacknowledged. We shall be pleased to make the necessary amendments in future editions of the book.

Printed and bound in Spain by Mateu Como, S.A.

2003
10 9 8 7 6